After Identity

Jonathan Rutherford

After Identity

Jonathan Rutherford

Lawrence & Wishart
LONDON 2007

Lawrence and Wishart Limited
99a Wallis Road
London
E9 5LN

First published 2007

Copyright © Lawrence and Wishart 2007

British Library Cataloguing in Publication Data.

A catalogue record for this book is available from the British Library

ISBN 978 1905007 400

Text setting Fran Davies

Printed and bound by Biddles, Kings Lynn

'We humanize what is going on in the world and in ourselves only by speaking of it, and in the course of speaking of it we learn to be human.'

Hannah Arendt

CONTENTS

Introduction

Here we are

In Michael Collins book *The Keepers of Truth* (Scribner, 2001), Bill lives a life of uneventful, quiet desperation, alone in a mansion on the edge of a decaying town in the mid West of the US. He works as a journalist on the local paper and is bewitched by a desire to speak the truth. It erupts from him and into print, much to the chagrin of his boss and the consternation of the local citizens. 'I got this tunnel vision, felt suddenly buried under the debris of our dead industrialism. We were occupying one of the gaps in history that go undocumented, that long silent stupefaction before some other means of survival comes along to save civilization.'

Here we are in our own gap in history. Old states of life no longer feel tenable, but what is to come in the future? We live in an afterlife of the post-modern and post-industrial. There is little that is tangible to give us our bearings. Zygmunt Bauman characterises this life as liquid modernity. It is a society of increasingly individualised individuals, which cannot easily hold its shape – it neither fixes nor binds time and space. Fluids flow and yield to the slightest pressure. They drip, flow, gush, swirl, disperse into particles, gather into a flood.[1] When we try and grasp the meaning of society, understanding escapes us like water.

In this liquid modern world our anchor is the culture we can create and which we can share. Bauman argues that we are each instructed to create our own biographical exit from this 'socially concocted mess', but this is an impossible task without recourse to the linguistic tools and cultural artefacts of our interdependency. We need others in order to make narratives which give meaning to our individual selves.

How shall we find the common shared meanings that connect us to others? If they no longer exist, how shall we make them? This predicament is not a new one. At the beginning of the twentieth century Georg Simmel described modernity as a culture of unrest. Individuals are alienated from one another, not by isolation, but because they have become anonymous in the public realm. Things without monetary value are ignored and margin-alised. The meaning of life slips through our fingers. For Weber capitalist modernity is an iron cage of 'specialists without spirit, sensualists without heart'. It is a nullity, which nevertheless 'imagines it has attained a level of civilization never before achieved'.

Rainer Marie Rilke struggles with this nullity in his sequence of poems *Duino Elegies* (1923). He searches for words which will express his feeling that something profound in his life is missing. He wants to grasp life and to express it in his art. He seeks solitude, which will allow him the inward contemplation of his imagination. But to communicate this inner world requires feeling, and his feelings are dependent upon his relationships with others. His need of others threatens his art, and yet his art means nothing without them. He cannot find the words to describe what it is he does want. He is caught up in an ambivalence that slides between need and desire. When Rilke looks at himself it is as an object through the eyes of another. He is a spectator of his life: 'Who, therefore, has turned us around, so that/ no matter what we do, we're in that attitude of someone leaving?'

Rilke's ambivalence resonates with our own liquid modern consumer society. It seduces us with the promise that we can become 'anybody we like'. But this is an impossible freedom. The pursuit of being anybody excludes the possibility of being ourselves. In three decades the size of our economy has almost doubled, we are richer than ever before – and yet this good life of acquisition and desire has not provided a collective sense of well being. Economic growth has brought with it inequality, insecurity and unprece-dented levels of household debt. The penetration of market relations into the social fabric of our lives marginalises human need. Dependency is a source of shame. We are beset by social problems that are individualised and hidden away from public view – depression, mental ill health, loneliness. Here we are, free consumers, inundated with choice, 'singing in our chains'.

After Identity is an attempt to find common shared meanings in response to this individualised and increasingly commercialised society. The opening chapter argues that in the last thirty years the influences of markets and neo-liberal ideology have accelerated the historical transformation of the social category of the individual. Identity was central to the liberation politics of the late 1960s social movements. Their collective activity of self-determination and self-realisation was organised around the differences of race, gender and sexuality. Their cultures of self affirmation created social value and political power and were taken up by other constituencies – for example people with disabilities and mental illness. They contributed to transformations in personal and moral consciousness. But the social movements, and the wider revolutionary left politics they sprang from, did not succeed in radically changing society. Today the languages and practices of identity are no longer associated with the emancipatory struggle for political agency and an interdependent individuality. The political expression of association has given way to the commercial market value of individualised rational choice. This ideal of being a consumer – unconstrained, choice-driven and self-reliant – has entangled identity in the exchange value of the market. It has become a more privatised and individualised affair.

Today we face a doubtfulness about what the striving to be ourselves is for. What does it mean to feel a sense of self-fulfilment? Consumer culture and its tantalising promises offers a panacea to fend off this uncertainty. But its effects can be corrosive, because it reconstitutes social activities and relations between people as market relations between individuals and things. The process of commodification leads to an isolating world inhabited by men and women whose social bonds are displaced or depleted. Like shoppers hunting for a bargain, we do not want to be distracted from pursuing our own elusive desire. Consumer culture glamorises and idealises our desire, splitting it off from our emotional need and our dependence on others. Desire is the idiom of our aliveness, but desire without a qualifying and balancing attachment to others casts us into a pursuit of the unattainable. Hovering in the wings are the new social threats of invisibility, meaninglessness, failure.

By entangling identity in market transactions and commodification, consumer culture has turned it against the individual. Identity is mobilised not only to enhance the exchange value of identity–confirming commodities, but also to increase productivity at work. Work has become an intimate part of our psychology as we market our personalities, compete with our peers for recognition, and constantly measure our performance against an ever-shifting and frequently unpredictable set of criteria. In this translucent world, success can be ephemeral. Its achievement lacks clearly defined means and ends. It is no longer simply about accumulating money and purchasing status. Nor is it straightforwardly about being functionally more effective, or more powerful than other people. Success is achieved by the identities we are capable and willing to make ourselves into. The apotheosis of this fabricating of identity is celebrity culture, in which success is about the light of recognition illuminating a person's unique singularity. Failure means a loss of identity – disappearing from the sight of others and becoming invisible.

The first chapter of the book, 'After identity', explores some of the ethical resources that might help an engagement with these current predicaments of identity. It argues that we need a better account of how we define human being, and of the changing dynamic between individuality and society, through which identities are made and remade. It asks what, in rethinking the idea of the individual, might come after identity. The origin of this question lies in the cultural theory of difference and identity. This theory is highly sophisticated in its explanation of the relational nature of identities. It has challenged Enlightenment rationality and its claim to speak for an undifferentiated humanity, exposing its operations of exclusion and opening up spaces for identities that were denied inclusion in its realm. But to ensure its own internal coherence, cultural theory concentrated on the construction of meaning in language and representation. It could not address the economic categories of class, the material nature of the body, or emotional life. To answer the question about what might come after identity we need to look elsewhere.

The chapter on 'Ghosts' examines the way memory and the heritage industry construct historical time and shape our understanding of white English national identity and 'race' difference. The narratives, ideologies, metaphors and fantasies of heritage fuse together the present and past into an undifferentiated union. Heritage becomes the attempt to make sense of the past without disturbing the social and symbolic order of the present. It is like an act of mourning while denying a death. In its attempts to bring the past back to life, heritage represents a loss that cannot be accepted and must continually be returned to. Our subjective sense of self is constructed around a national identity that manufactures ghosts – the dead who cannot settle but who prowl ceaselessly looking for release. This essay asks how we might find a way to face the future with less investment in maintaining differences and with a greater sense of hopefulness.

'Fallen among thieves' is about asylum seekers and how they are treated by the settled population, continuing the theme of identity and belonging. Refugees, asylum seekers, economic migrants, by their presence remind us of change and disruption. They need resources and they need help, and so invite envy, rage and suspicion. And yet, for all their apparent strangeness, if we who are settled are willing to look, we will recognise in them something familiar to our own lives. Migrants symbolise the paradox of modernity, the historic opportunity to make a life for one's self, but at the same time the experiencing of a loss of security, familiarity, home. We need not have experienced real homelessness and exile to feel the displacement and disorientation which pervades modern life. Like 'Ghosts', the essay concludes with the ethical impulse of reaching beyond our individual identity toward the other: an ethic of hospitality in which we each make ourselves someone's neighbour.

After Identity draws on a range of theoretical and philosophical resources in an attempt to rethink the nature of the individual and identity: the ideas of group analysis and one of its founding figures, the sociologist Norbert Elias; the philosophical work of Hannah Arendt and Martin Heidegger; the Christian-influenced thinking of Paul Ricoeur and Charles Taylor; the sociology of Zygmunt Bauman. What these all share in common is an endeavour to understand what it means to be human in society, with all that is problematic about this term. The essays in *After Identity* have been a process of thinking about a new kind of humanism. It is one which is constituted out of the recognition of our singularity and difference, not in a denial of it. It does not believe in the essential nature of anything. It is a humanism without guarantees, to borrow from Stuart Hall's phrase. As Hannah Arendt describes it, 'the conditions of human existence – life itself, natality and mortality, worldliness, plurality, and the earth – can never "explain" what we are or answer the question of who we are, for the simple reason that they never condition us absolutely.'[2]

It is this 'humanism without guarantees' that informs the final three essays. 'At war' is about masculinity and violence. It gives a brief historical appraisal of the changing relationship of individual males to the social structures that have shaped gendered behaviour and constrained violence. The 1960s and 1970s were a period when changes to men as a gender were encapsulated in a paradigmatic shift from the historical ideal of manliness, rooted in traditions of patriarchy, to the idea of masculinity. This informalisation of conventional behaviour was a response to the rigid demands made on both men and women to constrain, inhibit and modify their instinctual life and emotions. It has had a number of consequences. One of these relates to a pervasive anxiety about mortality. Where once death was feared but invested with a spiritual significance or social function, informalisation has uprooted socially embodied structures of sacred meaning and left individuals alone to their fate. In post-industrial societies, death has been removed to the horizon of living, where it hovers just out of sight. As a consequence, it is lived as a state of perpetual anxiety without beginning or ending. It is this amorphous unfocused fear that has helped to fuel the global militarisation of the War on Terror. The enemy is everywhere and nowhere.

'Earthbound' continues with the question about the value of human life that is raised in the concluding pages of 'At war'. It does this by interrogating our understanding of human biological existence and its relationship to the earth's living systems. Climate change has brought into question the collective future of humanity. Humanism needs an ecological ethic that will reframe the individual as part of the earth's ecology and so create a new relationship to nature. After identity there is the ethical experience of becoming who we are in connectedness with the living and non-living systems that have created us. Individuals are not born free. We make ourselves free, and we do so not in isolation from others but in relation to them, and also in relation to the plants and animals that sustain us. Our life-promoting, mortality-evading consumer societies have come to fear nature as the death which awaits us. The idea of becoming earthbound is to accept mortality, finitude and limitation in our lives.

Ending is the theme of the final chapter on the revolution in longevity. The old suffer from invisibility. They share the same street, live in the same block of flats, but they merge unnoticed into the hinterland of our gaze. Deprived of recognition, the old endure the same silence and invisibility that surrounds the dying. The cultural revolution in ageing is an historic opportunity to begin living well another stage of life. But beneath the growing abundance of promotional gloss and media hype, the future of ageing for the world majority is destined to be a time of financial insecurity, exclusion and poverty. The contemporary reforms to the pension system are examples of a political struggle over which classes of which generations will secure future surpluses of capital. Capitalism sells us an idea of old age that ignores those who can't afford it, and generates a fearful denial of decline, infirmity and death for those who can. We need alternative ways to live the third age, that can provide pleasure and opportunities for all, but are also able to acknowledge that life can only be incomplete. Dreams are invariably unrealised. Such sentiments are the nightmare of consumer culture, which responds to mortality with embarrassed silence. But in accepting the constraints of life, we might achieve the kind of fulfilment and well being that currently eludes us.

After Identity is a series of essays that attempt to look beyond the flux of social forms and identities to glimpse what might emerge in their wake. How do we create cultures and meaning able to bridge Bill's gap in history? We might begin by attending to the 'madness of unshared meanings'. As Wendy Wheeler describes it, these are the disorderly profusion of signs that have not yet been dragooned into the rule-bound semiotic system.[3] This is the world of the imagination, which has been expunged from official forms of knowledge. As Giorgio Agamben writes, 'Nothing can convey the extent of the change that has taken place in the meaning of experience so much as the resulting reversal of the status of the imagination.'[4] In antiquity the imagination had been the supreme medium of knowledge, the intermediary between the senses and the intellect. Today, he argues, it has been expropriated by modern rationalist forms of knowledge (p25).

There is something more to each of us that cannot easily be defined in language and representation, and there is also within us something that remains unfinished and open to the world. We can never be reduced entirely to sociological explanation. This is the intangible resource that leads us into the unknown, and which enables new kinds of collective political imagination to emerge. Here we are, 'in the manner of someone leaving', unsure of our destination.

NOTES

1. Zygmunt Bauman, *Liquid Modernity*, Polity 2005.

2. Hannah Arendt, *The Human Condition*, University of Chicago Press 1998, p11.

3. Wendy Wheeler, *The Whole Creature: Complexity, Biosemiotics and the Evolution of Culture*, Lawrence & Wishart 2006.

4. Giorgio Agamben, *Infancy & History*, trans. Liz Heron, Verso 1993, p24.

one | After identity

"This wishing to live together is silent, generally unnoticed, buried; one does not remark its existence until it falls apart"

Paul Ricoeur[1]

The café in an affluent area of North London was filled with well dressed men and women drinking coffee and passing the time of day in conversation. Many were sitting out at tables, covered over by an awning. Despite it being winter, the sun was shining and it was unusually warm. Someone was playing a penny whistle and as I walked past I noticed a hat in the middle of the pavement. To the left of the awning and keeping himself hidden was a young black man playing a traditional English folk song. His clothes were worn and he was wearing a pair of broken trainers on his feet. His face had the look of someone suffering a mental illness, or maybe it was just careworn from hardship. Two small children took money from their father and ran across to the hat to drop in their gift.

The young man's poverty and the abundance of the white, middle-class clientele sitting at their leisure around the café tables is a disparity that one witnesses in London every day. The scene was an enactment of the class and race relations that have shaped our society. The poor dependent on the largesse of the wealthy. History repeating itself in this fragment of post-colonial relations from an empire whose loss still cannot be acknowledged. Tradition being remade as the redemptive song of Olde England moves elsewhere, its cultural migration revealing a sense of displacement and uncertainty characteristic of our affluent society. The identities of the people involved served to create a tableau of contemporary England. It is a familiar conjuncture much analysed in the cultural studies of difference and identity, and yet I think it is one that escapes the ability of cultural theory to fully grasp.

Cultural theory developed its critique of identity politics partly in reaction to the legacy of the 'expressive humanism' of Richard Hoggart and Edward Thompson, and to the ideas of Raymond Williams.[2] These humanistic theories of identity relied on the idea of 'experience' and a unitary subject who existed prior to social relations and signification. In contrast, cultural theory, heavily influenced by structuralism, described subjectivity as the product of discourse, ideology, language. Experience was an illusion. The conditions of one's existence could only be 'lived' 'through the categories, classifications and frameworks of culture'.[3] This 'linguistic turn' opened up for interrogation the cultural and social construction of identity. It analysed identity as contingent upon its historical and political circumstances, with no essential or positive meaning in itself. The meaning of an identity was derived from its difference to other identities. This cultural theorising of difference was highly sophisticated in its explanation of the relational nature of identities. But to ensure its own internal coherence it concentrated on the construction of meaning in language and representation. It was not able to address the economic categories of class, the material nature of the body, or emotional life. The subject was divested of agency. For example, Foucault's 'end of man' and Althusser's Lacanian-inspired theory of ideology effectively dissolved individuals as active participants in culture and history.[4]

The cultural theorising of difference provided an effective demolition of Enlightenment humanism and its claim to speak for an undifferentiated humanity. It exposed its operations of exclusion and opened up spaces for those identities that had been denied inclusion in its realm. But in the process, it deracinated the subject from the planes of existence which might define human being – corporeal, emotional life (*zoe*), and 'ways of life' (*bios*).[5] French and French-inspired traditions of anti-humanism provided an oppositional stance against the bourgeois individual, but their rhetoric could not conceal the fact that they offered few serious challenges to the existing order of things. Anti-humanist theories of the subject, for all their brilliant deconstructive power, lacked the ethical resources to generate new, more egalitarian social relationships and identities to replace those they sought to undo. Their highly rationalised modes of knowledge and their intent to tease apart the existing fabric of meaning, echoed the calculative logic of the resurgent liberal market capitalism of the 1980s, which disaggregated public and traditional identities and communities.

In the last thirty years, the increasing influences of markets and neo-liberal ideology have transformed the social category of the individual. The individual struggle to create a personal identity has become the defining paradigm of how we live in Western cultures: we are called upon to invent our own identity and live in our own way and be true to ourselves. It is the means by which individuals struggle to give themselves meaning and representation. Questions of identity and meaning have been the site of historic struggles against racism, misogyny and homophobia. But, once defined by the new social movements as emancipation from the prejudice and constraints of the old order, identity has now been co-opted by the commercial market value of individual rational choice. Identity has become a more privatised and individualised affair, increasingly defined by social standing and the purchasing of status-giving positional goods. The value of positional goods diminishes as more people acquire them, however, creating a spiralling of consumption as people strive to maintain their status and identity. To fuel this dynamic and boost demand, finance capitalism has managed to disconnect consumer desire from individual available earnings by aggressively selling consumer credit. In July 2004, consumer debt exceeded £1 trillion in Britain, of which £183.6 billion was unsecured debt on personal loans, credit and store cards.[6] Making an identity has become entangled with commodity relations and the process of capital accumulation. It has become a costly business. Even for the relatively affluent, debt has reduced many to a state of indentured consumption and a future tied to unremitting work.

Caestroën / Flemming

The neo-liberal economic order has depoliticised the agency of identity by reconstituting social activities and relations between people as market relations between individuals and things. Price and proxies of price displace values of association and solidarity as the means of governing people. Individuals might feel empowered as consumers, but as citizens they feel unable to effect any kind of meaningful change. The social nature of individual relationships is undermined and the social ties and trust that constitute the public realm are broken apart. Individual self interest begins to predominate over social responsibility and the idea of a common good. Market-based reforms promote individual rational choice over democratic government. Consumerism's revolt against deference has challenged paternalism, but society has yet to find new democratic values and modes of authority; not only in the realm of politics, but also in cultural and family life. As choice multiplies, from consumer markets to public services, risk and responsibility shift from the state and business onto individuals. It becomes increasingly difficult to make meaningful decisions. Is it the optimum choice and the right one for us? What criteria should we use for making the judgement? However much we accumulate in the way of worldly goods, there remains an anxiety about 'something which is nothing'. What is left that is durable and trustworthy? We need to think about where we might find the moral and intellectual resources to understand and engage with these social and cultural changes. This essay is an attempt to think about the way the dynamic between individuality and society has changed over the last three decades. Identities are made in this dynamic. In rethinking the idea of the individual, what might come after identity?

How we live now

I was using a Barclays Bank cash machine, my card was ejected, and as I waited for the money a strap line flashed up on the screen: 'Open the door to your dreams'. My money rolled out and then it was gone, replaced by the image of an open door. It reminded me of a Lloyds Bank leaflet which read: 'How can we help you live your life?' Capitalism offers us more than material goods. It promises us the good life – dreams, hope, love, a secure

future. It has provided majorities in the industrialised countries with historically unprecedented levels of affluence and individual choice. In the last
thirty years, Gross Domestic Product has almost doubled in the UK. In the
last fifty years national income has tripled. But this economic growth has
not brought with it an increased satisfaction with our lives. The insecurities
and impermanence of consumer culture and the penetration of market
relations into the social fabric of people's lives has generated a set of 'post-
material' social problems – widespread mental ill health, systemic loneliness, growing numbers of psychologically damaged children, eating
disorders, obesity, alcoholism, drug addiction, compulsions to shop, spend
and accumulate things.

In 2004 Richard Layard advised the UK government that the total
economic cost of mental illness in Britain is an annual £25 billion – over 2
per cent of GDP.[7] The Mental Health Foundation put the figure at £93
billion a year, in lost productivity, health care spending and reductions in
quality of life.[8] Stress, anxiety and depression account for a third of all
working days lost. As alcohol-related deaths continue to increase, the
conservative estimate of the cost to the NHS of alcohol-related conditions
is as much as £1.7 billion per annum.[9] 'Mental disorders' are now among the
leading causes of world disease and disability. The World Health
Organisation predicts that by 2020 depression will rank second behind
heart disease as a 'leading cause of the global disease burden'.[10] We are living
in a social recession. Its symptoms and its pain are often concealed inside
our homes, where we experience them as our own shameful and personal
failings.

Available evidence shows that the global rate of mental ill health is
highest amongst young people, notably in the industrialised countries.
While 17 per cent of 1-15 year olds in war torn, poverty-stricken Ethiopia
are suffering from mental ill health, in Germany the figure is 20 per cent of
12-15 year olds and in the USA it is 21 per cent of 9-17 year olds.[11] In
Britain, the Nuffield Foundation have identified a sharp decline in the
mental health of teenagers.[12] Behavioural problems amongst adolescents
have more than doubled over the last twenty-five years. Nuffield Deputy

Director Sharon Witherspoon commented: 'This is not a trend which is driven by a small number of kids who are getting worse ... but a more widespread malaise.'[13] This social recession is dispersed across the British population. A survey on sleep undertaken by the Future Foundation revealed that one in four people in the UK were finding it increasingly difficult to sleep well. The biggest cause of sleep disorders is anxiety. Women coping with paid work, housework and childcare suffer more than men. The survey's manager, Brian Garvey, in an attempt to explain the findings, said: 'Fear has become a powerful tool in society. A nervousness permeates our current lives.' [14]

Stress, depression, breakdown, bullying, violence might appear to have their source in a dysfunctional individual, but they are dysfunctions that belong to their wider social networks. Social life is not external to inner psychological reality; its matrix of conscious and unconscious communications form the innermost being of individual personality. Shame, failure, feelings of worthlessness, hopelessness and meaninglessness are our modern dreads, and they arise in the class and social relations that we grow up in. After three decades of the neo-liberal economic order, we are a society that is beset by loss; loss of belonging, loss of political purchase on the world, loss of hope. We live in a paradox. We are collectively, politically inert, yet we exist in a state of continuous activity, whipped on by the exhortation to be 'hard working families'. Companies are re-engineered, institutions re-configured, departments re-organised, working practices reviewed, schools repeatedly inspected, employees monitored and appraised. Goals, visions and mission statements are invented and re-defined. Politicians urge us to join the enterprise culture, become more business-like, embrace change. But in reality, this dynamic of permanent change simply reproduces the status quo. Nothing actually, meaningfully, changes. In this social recession, there is no politics to give voice to our protest. There is no alternative which offers a better future that is more equal, more just, more tolerant, and more kind.

Richard Easterlin was one of the first economists to study statistics on the reported levels of happiness in society. He concluded that in the USA:

'higher income was not systematically accompanied by greater happiness.'[15] Andrew Oswald investigated this claim and looked at the evidence indicating satisfaction with life in Europe since 1973. The results, he suggests, broadly bear out Easterlin's conclusions. They counter the idea that 'better economic performance means more happiness for a nation':[16] 'Reported levels of "satisfaction with life" in Europe are only slightly higher than they were twenty years ago.'[17] The trend is confirmed by the measures of subjective well being (SWB), which assess the psychological state of the population, for example personal development and self fulfilment. These have shown little movement over the last thirty years.[18] As Richard Reeves writes: 'Crudely put, above a certain point – around $15,000 a head Gross Domestic Product – more growth stops delivering more happiness.'[19] In its 2004 report on economic insecurity the International Labour Organisation concludes that 'wealth, it seems, does not beget security'.[20] To assess the validity of these claims, the New Economics Foundation (NEF) invented the Measure of Domestic Progress (MDP). The MDP adjusts conventional economic measures such as GDP and consumer expenditure to include social and environmental costs and benefits: for example the costs of crime are usually excluded from the accounting framework. The NEF's MDP mirrored the findings of Easterlin and Oswald: 'life satisfaction is resolutely static in spite of continuing economic growth.'[21]

The neo-liberal economic order

The experience is not historically unique. The promise of modernity has always lain in the dream of a better future. The idea of progress was the bourgeois ideology of nineteenth-century liberal capitalism. Defer gratification and accumulate capital. Innovate, build, expand the empire. A better world lies ahead for our nation. But as the economist Joseph Schumpeter has argued, capitalism is a system whose dynamic requires a perpetual anticipation of futures which never arrive. Schumpeter defines capitalism as 'a method of economic change' which can never be stationary.[22] Liberal market capitalism is not concerned with administering existing structures but with creating and destroying them, constantly revolutionising itself from within in a process of 'creative destruction'. This dynamic of innovation seeks out non-market spheres of life to commodify. Liberal market capitalism continuously creates and dismantles identities, making social life precarious.

Progress in the eighteenth and nineteenth centuries was driven by capital accumulation. It precipitated a mass exodus from the land and the growth of poverty-stricken industrial conurbations. As the market expanded, it enclosed the commons, transforming land and labour into commodities that could be produced for sale on the market. By the 1820s the creed of economic liberalism had become the organising principle of a society engaged in creating a market economy. Liberalism stood for free trade, a market in labour and the international commodification of money (the gold standard). The transformation of society into a market economy meant that increasing areas of life were subject to the rule of price. Georg Simmel, writing at the end of the nineteenth century, described modernity as a culture of unrest. It meant that 'the core and meaning of life slips through our fingers again and again, that definitive satisfactions become ever rarer, that all the effort and activity is not actually worthwhile'.[23] The point of life is forever yet to come.

People's traditional ways of life, their social interactions and settled institutional arrangements were brutally uprooted by the logic of the market. Each man, woman and child of the emerging working class was transmogrified into a commodity. Industrial capitalism and its political repression, workhouses and brutal penal system gave rise to widespread political opposition. According to Karl Polanyi, this countermovement 'was more than the usual defensive behaviour of a society faced with change; it was a reaction against a dislocation which attacked the fabric of society, and which would have destroyed the very organization of production that the market had called into being'.[24] The nineteenth-century countermovement gave birth to cultural, religious and political traditions that aimed to socialise capitalism and set limits to the expansion of markets into social and cultural domains of life. In the years after World War 11 this counter movement managed to achieve a consensus for regulating markets and for the state provision of public goods. But it was not to last. In reaction there emerged a creed of <u>neo-liberalism which resurrected the liberal market ideology of the nineteenth century.</u>

 <u>The neo-liberal economic order</u> began to be constructed thirty years ago in Britain with the election of the 1979 Conservative government. Policies were introduced that attempted to cut the growing costs of the welfare state and to reverse the decline in the profitability of British capitalism. The philosophy of neo-liberalism was summed up in Margaret Thatcher's now infamous pronouncement: 'I don't believe in society. There is no such thing, only individual people, and their families.'[25] Her chief influence was F.A Hayek, whose *Road to Serfdom* was the foundational text of neo-liberalism. Democratic socialism, which had been the utopia of the last few generations, was unachievable. Its ideals of social justice, greater equality and security could only be achieved by a planned economy which abolished private enterprise and ownership. This collectivism would involve the arbitrary and coercive intervention of authority, privileging equality at the expense of freedom. The individual must be set free. This neo-liberal version of individualism is defined in Milton Friedman's *Capitalism and Freedom*: 'A liberal is fundamentally fearful of concentrated power. His objective is to preserve the maximum degree of freedom for each individual separately that is compatible with one man's freedom not interfering with other men's freedom. He believes that this objective requires that power be dispersed. He is suspicious of assigning to government any functions that can be performed through the market.'[26] Only the free market of 'competitive capitalism' can ensure the separation of political power and economic power and so guarantee human liberty against the encroachment of state collectivism. Neo-liberalism was an ideological project that would reshape state institutions, create a new consumer culture of individual choice and liberalise economic activity in order to shift the balance of political forces back in favour of capital.

Neo-liberal ideas had begun to gain influence amongst right-wing politicians and policy-makers in the 1960s. The US economy, ascendant in the post-war years, now had to compete with lower cost producers in

Western Europe and Japan. The result was a glut on the world market and a decline in the rates of profit. In 1973 the cartel of oil producing countries (OPEC) significantly increased oil prices. Inflation rose to double figures. Growth in output, investment, productivity and wages slowed. The value of exports decreased while the price of imports increased. The OPEC countries, awash in revenue from their oil exports, invested in the US financial markets, creating a large surplus of 'petro-dollars' which were then loaned out to those national economies struggling to correct their balance of payments deficit. This set in place a cycle of debt crises which undermined nation state control over national economies and which was to continue into the new century.

The emerging globalised economy decisively shifted power to the financial markets. The World Bank and the IMF were captured by neo-liberal ideologues and put into the service of US economic interests. By 1976, a Labour government in Britain was presiding over an ailing and indebted British economy. It had already abandoned the economic priority of full employment and replaced it with monetary policies to control rising inflation. In order to secure an IMF loan of £3 billion it agreed to cut public expenditure by £2.5 billion. In total, public expenditure would be cut by £4 billion. The loan was the symbolic end of the Labour Party's brand of social democracy. It marked a historical defeat for the counter movement to liberal capitalism.

With the election of a Conservative government in 1979 neo-liberalism set the agenda for change. High interest rates and austerity measures were introduced to shut down high-cost, low-profit means of production. Capital controls were abolished. The welfare state began to be dismantled. Mass unemployment was used as an economic instrument to drive down labour costs and undermine the bargaining power of the trade unions. The process of de-industrialisation reduced full-time manufacturing employment amongst men and increased the numbers of female workers in less secure, part-time service jobs. The decline in labour market security created involuntary part-time employment and disguised unemployment. The liberalisation of the money markets with the 'Big Bang' in 1986 allowed an extraordinary global expansion of capital. It was aided by the deregulation of domestic public sectors and the privatisation of public utilities of water, gas, electricity and telecoms. New services markets were created out of previously public sector domains in response to the overcapacity and falling rate of profit in the international manufacturing sector.

These new regimes of accumulation, and the consumer cultures they have created, represent a new historical phase in the history of capitalist development. They have significantly shifted political influence and resources away from organised labour and fractured the old industrial social order. The conservative scholar Francis Fukuyama argues that the three decades between 1965 and 1995 experienced rates of change unlike those in previous historical periods. 'The rate of change in a variety of social indicators has been so great that this period deserves to be characterised as a "Great Disruption" in earlier patterns of social life.' [27] From a left perspective, Immanuel Wallerstein takes a longer-term historical view. Compared to the progress of the nineteenth century, the twentieth century 'has been a roller coaster'. Advances in technology have outstripped the science fiction fantasies of the Victorians. The rate and scale of capital accumulation has been beyond their wildest dreams. Wallerstein also argues that the democratisation of societies across the world could not have been predicted by nineteenth-century democrats. 'Yet as we all know, in the twenty-first century we are surrounded by fear, confusion, desperate scrambling again by all and sundry.' [28] The ever faster growth of capitalism has 'gotten out of hand'. We are faced with uncertainty and we find it politically and psychologically difficult to handle. Wallerstein's future is not one of unfolding progress, but a period of transition in which the outcome remains 'extremely uncertain'. [29]

The ideal of individual self determined freedom, as promised by neo-liberalism, has not been realised in the world it has brought into existence. The official version of the last thirty years insists that economic progress has made everyone better off. Globalisation has spread wealth and opportunities around the world. The evidence does not bear this out. Contrary to the utopian expectations of the neo-liberals, markets in capitalism do not tend toward equilibrium, nor do they operate under conditions of perfect competition. The new deregulated markets in labour, finance, trade and services which emerged in the 1980s did not arise spontaneously. They required a huge increase in political control, regulation and intervention. The apparently greater degrees of personal self-expression offered by consumer culture coincided with new forms of standardisation in which the rhetoric of the market – the supremacy of personal choice, the inviolability of individual ambition – disguised the growing inequalities between rich and poor. Furthermore, neo-liberal policies did not succeed in improving economic performance. UK productivity continues to lag behind France and Germany. In the US, argues Robert Brenner, economic performance in wages and productivity during the period 1995-2000 'barely matched the levels achieved in the 25-year period between 1948 and 1973'. By 2000 'real hourly wages for production and non-supervisory workers were still palpably below, and the poverty rate above, their 1973 bests'.[30] His view is supported by a group of researchers at the US Center for Economic Policy and Research, who compared the twenty years of globalisation between 1980 and 2000 with the previous two decades, 1960-1980. They used standard measures of progress in the categories of economic growth, health outcomes and education for all countries where the data was available. Their report concludes: 'the results are overwhelmingly in one direction: in every category, the comparisons show diminished progress overall in the period of globalisation as compared with the prior two decades.' [31]

In Britain liberal market capitalism has created historically high levels of inequality. In the last fifteen years the number of billionaires has nearly tripled. In 2005 an average chief executive was paid 113 times more than an average worker. Between 1980 and 1999, the richest 1 per cent of the UK population increased its share of national income from around 6 per cent to 13 per cent.[32] This tiny elite owns 25 per cent of the UK's marketable wealth. In contrast, 50 per cent of the population shared only 6 per cent of total wealth.[33] Exclude housing from these estimates, and inequality increases even further. Fifty per cent of families have £600 or less in savings, and 25 per cent are £200 or more in debt.[34] Inequality not only damages the life chances of people living in poverty. It adversely affects the quality of life of everyone. Inequality of status is a cause of ill health and decreases individual life expectancy – a five to ten year difference between social classes. Research reveals that life expectancy is affected by psychological and social factors – even the comfortably off tend to have shorter lives than the very wealthy.[35] The social consequences of inequality are registered in the New Economic Foundation's Measure of Domestic Progress, which reached a peak in 1975. Through the 1980s, as GDP began to rise rapidly, MDP fell consistently. The web of social and institutional relations that held people together has been fragmented by the neo-liberal economic order.

Neo-liberalism as a political creed cannot realise its own ideal of individual freedom. Its reliance on the market to distribute liberty destroys the social relations necessary for its flourishing. Its logic is to extend economic principles to all areas of life in order to maximise the reach of the market. Social values are displaced by price and proxies of price, for example targets and performance indicators. Cost benefit calculation takes precedence over social evaluative categories to become the method of governing individuals and populations. The relational nature of individuals is marginalised and discounted. The market generates social inequality, condemning individuals and communities to generations of poverty and social exclusion. Hayek evades the implications of these problems by arguing for a normative model of morality which will hold individuals together: 'I have said that liberty, to work well requires not merely the existence of strong moral convictions but also the acceptance of particular moral views.'[36] However these moral views do not extend to a concern for the common good. Neo-liberalism, with its lack of any sense of moral obligation to others, and its massive state interventions to enforce entrepreneurial and market shaped forms of life, begets an impoverished version of its own vision of liberty. It gives form to a 'market state' which, in Michel Foucault's words, develops both direct and indirect techniques for 'leading and controlling individuals without at the same time being responsible for them'. [37]

Common life

Confronted by the destructive impact of neo-liberalism, how are we to organise a democratic life in which individual self determination is balanced with the constraints imposed by our obligations toward others? In a culture of multiple and mobile identities that have become increasingly atomised by market society we need to rediscover our interdependence. Identity expresses our two greatest – and incompatible – wants in life: freedom and security. We desire to experience our individual life as unique and meaningful to ourselves, but we equally feel a need to belong to, and define ourselves through, broader collectives. It is in our relationships with others that we attempt to reconcile this paradox and find self-fulfilment. The ethical value of self-fulfilment and an authentic life has entered deep into modern Western consciousness, but the conditions for its realisation do not yet exist. Charles Taylor argues that it is a new phenomenon: 'There is a certain way of being human that is my way. I am called upon to live my life in this way, and not in imitation of anyone else's. But this gives a new importance to being true to myself. If I am not, I miss the point of my life, I miss what being human is for me.'[38]

Norbert Elias, in his essay 'The Society of Individuals', provides a framework for rethinking the dynamic between individuality and society. He remarks that the historical development of self-consciousness has led to a 'special satisfaction' that the individual 'owes everything he regards as unique and essential to himself, to himself alone, to his "nature", and to no one else'.[39] Elias dismisses the liberal orthodoxy that individuals are discrete 'closed personalities'. The pursuit of self-fulfilment and self-determination as an individualised project, subject only to rules of just conduct, is mistaken. Human beings are social and emotional beings who are fundamentally oriented toward and dependent upon other people through-out our lives. Elias defines this interrelationship with the word figuration:

> The network of interdependencies among human beings is what binds them together. Such interdependencies are the nexus of what is here called the figura-tion, a structure of mutually oriented and dependent people. As people are more

or less dependent on each other first by nature and then through social learning ... and socially generated reciprocal needs, they exist, one might venture to say, only as pluralities, only in figurations.[40]

What shapes, binds and gives meaning to an individual's belonging is 'the ineradicable connection between his desires and behaviours and those of other people, of the living, the dead, and even in a certain sense the unborn.'[41] We need to find a way of understanding our relationship to others – past, present and future – that acknowledges both our individuality and our social being. To this end Elias offers a revolution in our thinking.

> Only when the individual stops taking himself as the starting point of his thought, stops viewing the world like someone who looks from the 'interior' of his house on to the street 'outside', at the houses 'opposite', and is able – by a new Copernican revolution of his thought and feeling – to see himself and his shell as part of the street, to see them in relation to the whole mobile human network, only then will his feeling gradually fade that he is something isolated and self-contained 'inside', while the others are something separated from him by an abyss, a 'landscape', an 'environment', a society.[42]

In *The Human Condition*, Hannah Arendt provides some philosophical substance to Elias's sociology. She is interested in the fate of our common world. 'To live together in the world means essentially that a world of things is between those who have it in common.'[43] She likens the 'world of things' to a table around which people sit and which orders their relationships with one another. In the same way a common life both relates people to one another and separates them:

> The public realm, as the common world, gathers us together and yet prevents our falling over each other, so to speak. What makes mass society so difficult to bear is not the number of people involved, or at least not primarily, but the fact that the world between them has lost its power to gather them together, to relate and to separate them (pp52-53).

This loss of a common life is characterised by a 'worldlessness', in which individuals no longer share a concern with the same 'world of things' – 'the sameness of the object can no longer be discerned' (p58). Rather than leading to a diversity of identities and experiences, the consequence is the loss of 'things essential to a truly human life' (p58). 'Men have become entirely private, that is, they have been deprived of seeing and hearing others, of being seen and heard by them. They are all imprisoned in the subjectivity of their own singular experience' (p58). Arendt retains in her idea of a common world a religious notion of the sacred. In contrast, Martin Heidegger, who was such an important influence on her work, offers a more humanistic account of common life and its making. In his essay 'Building Dwelling Thinking', Heidegger describes how 'things' are the ordering of human being in the world.[44] Where Arendt uses the example of a table, Heidegger uses the analogy of a bridge: 'the bridge does not first come to a location to stand in it; rather, a location comes into existence only by virtue of the bridge' (p154). The bridge gathers to itself the elements of the world and in so doing brings into being a space and its boundaries. 'The boundary is that from which something begins its presencing' (p154). For Arendt the 'world of things' resides in God, but for Heidegger it is created in the mortal activity of building and dwelling: 'the way in which you are and I am, the manner in which we humans are on the earth, is Buan, dwelling' (p147).

For Heidegger, dwelling is the basic character of Being, or, to be more precise, the 'there' of Being – 'only if we are capable of dwelling, only then can we build' (p160). In reflecting on 'the state of dwelling in our precarious age', he argues that the problem is that individuals 'ever search anew for the nature of dwelling, that they must learn to dwell'. The human predicament is the plight of our worldlessness, and that we cannot dwell together in the world. In a further essay '... Poetically Man Dwells ...' Heidegger asks how we might understand the meaning of this dwelling.[45] The poetic, he says, 'is the basic capacity for human dwelling'. But what does Heidegger mean? Taking the title of his essay from a poem by Friedrich Hölderlin, he argues that an authentic poetry is the expression of an ontology of man's liking for man. Drawing on Hölderlin he describes authentic poetry as existing in the world of mortals so long as 'Kindness, The Pure ... still stays with his heart'. Kindness is Hölderlin's translation for the Greek word charis – 'For kindness it is, that ever calls for kindness' (p229). In Heidegger there is a search for a humanist religiosity of meaning and purpose in life.

The ethical and the political

The problems created by the neo-liberal economic order and the ways it has entangled the individual in the economic activity of consumption confront us with the need to remake a common life. Elias with his challenge to the conceit of individualisation offers us the concept of figuration to think about the interconnectedness of our social existence. Arendt presents us with an essentially religious idea of this commonality, one whose truths are the same for all, hence bringing into existence human society. Heidegger suggests a more humanist description of dwelling as the human creating of a common life, which finds its meaning in the idea of kindness. Each provides a thoughtfulness about the nature of our individual subjectivities. They offer an ethical language to describe anew the way we live in relation to others. Such an ethics requires a politics which gives it a sphere in which to operate, and which can contest the logic of capital accumulation.

There are three principles we have inherited which have defined the emancipatory claims of modernity: liberty, equality and fraternity. The right have traditionally laid claim to liberty, while the left have prioritised equality. Fraternity has never achieved the same ideological significance as the other two principles. It was the virtue of the political activist, and the ethos of the society promised by a utopian future. But the tradition of fraternity retains the potential to become a new narrative of the individual's relationship to society. Fraternity, in its recognition of human interdependence, is the catalyst which brings together liberty and equality. In its advocacy of the social and relational nature of human beings it implies that the self-fulfilment of each is indivisible from the equal worth of all. The philosopher Paul Ricoeur offers a way of thinking about the politics of fraternity and its relationship to ethical life and identity.

In *Oneself as Another*, Ricoeur begins his inquiry into ethical life by defining its 'ethical intention' as, 'the desire to live well with and for others in just institutions'.[46] He then examines the three points of this definition.

The first point is 'to live well', which means to follow the 'good life' or the 'true life'. He describes this in terms similar to those of Charles Taylor, as 'the nebulous of ideals and dreams of achievements with regard to which a life is held to be more or less fulfilled or unfulfilled' (p179). Taylor's ethic of self-fulfilment is a reflexive concern for one's own identity and self-esteem. But it is social rather than individualistic. It involves the right of everyone to achieve their own unique way of being human. To dispute this right in others is to fail to live within its own terms. Its relational nature leads Ricoeur to the second point: 'with and for others'. He describes living with and for others as 'solicitude'. Solicitude is not separate from individual self esteem: it expresses its social nature by unfolding its dialogic dimension. Ricoeur explains this by using the example of friendship in which 'each loves the other as being the man he is' (p183). To be 'equal among friends' is for two friends to render to the other 'a portion equal to what he or she receives' (p184). What follows on from the giving and receiving of friendship is the idea of equality. Friendship involves the ethic of reciprocity and this sets friendship on the path to justice: 'where life together shared by a few people gives way to the distribution of shares in a plurality on the scale of a historical, political community' (p188). Ricoeur is describing ethical life as originating in the sphere of interpersonal relationships and extending upward into the wider social realm and into the political community.

The aim of living necessitates an interdependency with others. The corollary of this interdependency is equality. Consequently, Ricoeur argues, the aim of living encompasses a sense of justice. This brings his inquiry to the third point of the 'ethical intention': 'just institutions'. Justice finds its expression in the idea of 'just institutions'. By institution Ricoeur means, 'the structure of living together as this belongs to a historical community'. The structure is irreducible to interpersonal relations and yet it is 'bound up with them in a remarkable sense' (p194). This is because institutions require political communities whose function is distributive. The distributive operations of a political community are more than the sharing implied by solicitude. Distribution involves the apportioning of 'roles, tasks, advantages and disadvantages between the members of a society' (p200). Where there is sharing there may be too much or not enough – 'the unjust man is the one who takes too much in terms of advantages or not enough in terms of burdens' (p201). Equality is the ethical core of justice. And it is not exclusive to the discourses of the political community. There is no wall between the individual and society which prevents the transition of the ethical aim from interpersonal life to the social world. Equality for Ricoeur 'is to life in institutions what solicitude is to interpersonal relations' (p202). Justice holds persons to be irreplaceable and so adds to solicitude, 'to the extent that the field of application of equality is all of humanity' (p202). In an interview Ricoeur summarises his notion of ethical life as: 'the wish for personal accomplishment with and for others, through the virtue of friendship and, in relation to a third party, through the virtue of justice'.[47] He offers a way of reinterpreting the ideal of fraternity as the ethical framing of political and economic relations and principles. From its old incarnation as a limited and gender biased expression of solidarity, it becomes a reparative ethic of common life.

After identity

We are faced with the diminishing of common life, and with it, a doubtfulness about the meaning of self-fulfilment. Insecurity generates the ubiquitous preoccupation with identity and the need to be recognised and affirmed. The question 'who am I?' reflects a need to know our place in the world and what we amount to in the eyes of others. It is an appeal for belonging to a name, and it requires validation through collective, social recognition. But in our individualised, consumer culture, its fate hinges on the market value it can fetch in an hierarchical economy of signs. It is no longer simply enough to assert one's identity toward recognition; in a market society one must pay to assert it through the acquisition of status and consumer goods. The commodification of identity intensifies our anxiety at finding ourselves with strangers in a world that holds no intrinsic meaning or purpose. Difference becomes a source of persecution. In the face of this 'nullity' and the paranoia it creates, there is no choice but to create ethical and political meaning: to face one another and persevere in our efforts to make contact and establish communication. The giving of recognition and the need to be recognised by others is fundamental to our existence. Recognition confirms our interdependency. It allows for the development of a dialectic between self and other in which difference can be acknowledged. 'The demand of identity', writes Ricoeur, 'always involves something violent with respect to others. On the contrary, the search for recognition implies reciprocity' (p60). There is nothing more in the world than individuals and what is between us. After identity there is ethical life, which is what we make out of what lies between. In this respect we are all always off centre, reaching out toward the other.

NOTES

1. Paul Ricoeur, *Critique and Conviction*, Polity Press, London 1998, p99.
2. See Colin Sparks, 'Stuart Hall, cultural studies and marxism', *Stuart Hall: Critical Dialogues in Cultural Studies*, David Morley and Kuan-Hsing Cen (eds), Routledge 1996, pp71-101.
3. Stuart Hall, 'Cultural Studies: two paradigms', *Media, Culture and Society*, 2, 1980, pp57-72.
4. Michel Foucault, *The Order of Things: An Archaeology of the Human Sciences*, Routledge 1986; Louis Althusser, 'Ideology and Ideological State Apparatuses', *Lenin and Philosophy*, New Left Books, London 1971.
5. See Hannah Arendt, *The Human Condition*, University of Chicago Press 1998; Giorgio Agamben, *Homo Sacer: Sovereign Power and Bare Life*, trans. Daniel Heller-Roazen, Stanford University Press 1995.
6. Credit Action, 'Debt Statistics', March 2005, www.creditaction.org.uk.
7. Richard Layard, *Mental Health: Britain's Biggest Social Problem?* www.strategy.gov.uk/downloads/files/mh_layard.pdf.
8. Mental Health Foundation, *Time for Public Mental Health: A briefing from the Mental Health Foundation in advance of the White Paper on Public Health, 2004*, www.mentalhealth.org.uk/html/content/briefing_white_paper_public_mh_1104.pdf.
9. Office of National Statistics (2005), 'Alcohol Related Deaths Rates continue to rise', www.statistics.gov.uk/CCI/nugget.asp?ID=1091&Pos=3&ColRank=1&Rank=19; Institute of Alcohol Studies, Fact Sheet, *Alcohol and Health*,

2005, p8, www.ias.org.uk.

10. WHO press release, *The World Health Report 2001*, 2001,
www.who.int/inf-pr-2001/en/pr2001-42.html.

11. World Health Organisation, *Child and Adolescent Mental Health Policies
and Plans*, World Health Organisation 2005, p8,
www.who.int/entity/mental_health/policy/en/Child%20%20Ado%20
Mental%20Health_final.pdf.

12. Stephan Collishaw, Barbara Maughan, Robert Goodman, Andrew Pickles,
'Time trends in adolescent mental health', *Journal of Child Psychology and
Psychiatry and Allied Disciplines*, Nov. 2004, Vol.45, no.8. pp 1350-1362. See
also The Nuffield Foundation, *2004 Seminars on Children and Families:
Evidence and Implications*, www.nuffieldfoundation.org/fileLibrary/pdf/
2004_seminars_childern_families_adolescents_and_wellbeing001.pdf.

13. Madeleine Bunting, 'Today's youth: anxious, depressed, antisocial', *The
Guardian*, 13.9.04.

14. Jamie Doward, 'A good sleep is an impossible dream as stress winds up
Britons', *The Observer*, 13.3.05, www.futurefoundation.net/Press%20
coverage.html.

15. Andrew Oswald, 'Happiness and Economic Performance', *Economic
Journal*, 107, 1997, www2.warwick.ac.uk/fac/soc/economics/staff/faculty/
oswald/happecperf.pdf.

16. Ibid, p15.

17. Ibid, p16.

18. New Economics Foundation (NEF), *Chasing Progress Beyond Measuring
Economic Growth, 2004*, p4, www.neweconomics.org/gen/well_being_ top.
aspx?page=1038&folder=174&

19. Richard Reeves, *The Politics of Happiness*, NEF, 2003, p8,
ww.neweconomics.org/gen/well_being_top.aspx?page=1038&folder=174&.

20. International Labour Office, 'Economic insecurity is a global crisis', 2004,
www.ilo.org/public/english/ protection/ses/download/docs/happiness.pdf.
See also www.ilo.org/ses.

21. New Economics Foundation, *Chasing Progress Beyond Measuring Economic
Growth*, op cit.

22. Joseph Schumpeter, *Capitalism, Socialism and Democracy*, Allen & Unwin
1976, p82.

23. Georg Simmel, 'Money in Modern Culture', *Theory, Culture and Society*,

Vol.8, 1991, p23.

24. Karl Polanyi, *The Great Transformation*, Beacon Press 1957, p130.

25. Margaret Thatcher, Interview, *Woman's Own*, 31.10.87.

26. Milton Friedman, *Capitalism and Freedom*, University of Chicago Press 1962, p39.

27. Francis Fukuyama, *The End of Order*, The Social Market Foundation 1997, p14.

28. Immanuel Wallerstein, *The Decline of American Power*, The New Press 2003, p43.

29. Ibid, p46.

30. Robert Brenner, 'Toward the Precipice', *London Review of Books*, 6.2.03, www.lrb.co.uk/v25/n03/bren01_.html.

31. Mark Weisbrot, Dean Baker, Egor Kraev and Judy Chen, *The Scorecard on Globalization 1980-2000: Twenty Years of Diminished Progress*, Center for Economic and Policy Research Briefing Paper, www.cepr.net/globalization/ scorecard_on_globalization.htm.

32. Institute of Public Policy Research, *The State of the Nation*, see Press Release: 'A decade of tackling poverty, but Britain's far from a fair society', August 2005, www.ippr.org.uk/press/index.php?release=332. See also: Will Paxton and Mike Dixon, *The State of the Nation: An Audit of Injustice in the UK*, IPPR 2004; Holly Sutherland, Tom Sefton and David Piachaud, *Poverty in Britain: The impact of government policy since 1997*, Joseph Rowntree Foundation, www.jrf.org.uk.

33. National Statistics, 'Share of the Wealth', www.statistics.gov.uk/cci/nugget.asp?id=2.

34. James Banks, Zoe Smith, Matt Wakefield, *The Distribution of Financial Wealth in the UK: Evidence from 2000 BHPS Data*, Institute of Fiscal Studies, WP02/21, 2002, p7, www.ifs.org.uk. See also: Mike Brewer et al. 'Poverty and Inequality in Britain: 2004', *Commentary 96*, www.ifs.org.uk.

35. See Richard Wilkinson's work on the relationship between inequality and health. For example: Richard Wilkinson, 'The Impact of Inequality: empirical evidence', *Renewal*, Vol. 14, No 1, 2006, www.renewal.org.uk.

36. F.A. Hayek, *Studies in Philosophy, Politics and Economics*, Routledge Kegan Paul 1978, p231.

37. Thomas Lemke, '"The birth of bio-politics": Michel Foucault's lecture at the College de France on neo-liberal governmentality', *Economy and*

Society, Vol. 30, No.2, May 2001, p201.

38. Charles Taylor, *The Ethics of Authenticity*, Harvard University Press 1997, pp28-29.

39. Norbert Elias, 'The Society of Individuals', in *The Society of Individuals*, Continuum 1991, p56.

40. Norbert Elias, *The Civilising Process*, Blackwell 1982, pp213-214.

41. Norbert Elias, 'The Society of Individuals', op cit, p43.

42. Ibid, p56.

43. Hannah Arendt, *The Human Condition*, University of Chicago Press 1998, p52.

44. Martin Heidegger, 'Building Dwelling Thinking', *Poetry, Language, Thought*, trans. Albert Hofstadter, Harper and Row 1975.

45. '... Poetically Man Dwells ...', in Heidegger op cit.

46. Paul Ricoeur, *Oneself as Another*, trans Kathleen Blamey, University of Chicago Press 1994, p180 (see also p172).

47. Paul Ricoeur, *Critique and Conviction*, Polity Press 1998, p92.

two | Ghosts

"The past has to 'wear out' before we can go on. And that applies not only to our personal lives, but to countries as well."

Cees Nooteboom[1]

Now and then

Haworth in Yorkshire was home to the Bronte sisters. It is now a heritage site dominated by the narrow lane which passes through the village, rising up the hill, lined with gift shops and tea houses. It is a caricature of Olde England, whose claim to authenticity lies in its displays of ersatz Victoriana, New Age products and Third World handicraft, which have become the ubiquitous emblems of the English idyll. The reason for the existence of this commerce and the visitors crowding the narrow lane window-shopping is hidden away behind the church, a surprisingly small and modest parsonage which, when I entered, had only a handful of visitors musing around its rooms. I had expected to be subjected to an overweening Bronte myth, but it was the pathos of their home and the story of their hard, closed and short lives that made the impression. A graveyard dominates the immediate surroundings. Its heavy, oppressive stones and slabs lend the place a dark foreboding of death. Returning to the small main street and the crowds enjoying the sunshine, it was as if this was the true heritage experience, a welcome distraction from the past hidden away in its deathly surroundings. Haworth represents heritage as a dislocation from history. An

slight/unreal similarity

opportunity to sidestep the reverberations of the past and enjoy the simulacrum.

The day out had been part of a journey up north with my partner to visit relatives. Such occasions bring the past into sharp relief. Memories of childhood are evoked by the changed urbanscape of what had once been home. The journey itself becomes a liminal experience, as a familiar, ordered, temporal living is disrupted. We began in Daubhill in Bolton, historically the immigrant area of the town, once inhabited by the Polish and Irish and now by the Asian community. The terraced housing was interspersed with the detritus of old mills and workshops. We had been looking for an early childhood home but all that survived of the street was a short length of cobbled stone which led into a rubbish-strewn strip of ground, trapped between the brick wall of what had once been the de Havilland factory and a new building which looked as if it housed an electricity generator. Across the road was the iron skeleton of a new mosque under construction, the emblem of a community establishing a permanent cultural landmark. It will soon displace the Catholic church down the hill, which had secured the presence of an earlier marginalised ethnic minority. The traces of a multitude of pasts and histories lay scattered everywhere; an auntie's old house, the ruin of a mill, the Co-op and library; like footprints they led back into previous ways of life now ended. Haworth is an example of how heritage can commodify the past and create a culture which denies decay and transience. But this wandering on foot through the narrow terraced streets of Daubhill made their traces both visible and real. The effect of their reverberation in the present is paradoxical. The past can be related to and in the process let go of and allowed to give way to emergent life. The signs of racial difference, English Islam, the gaudy structures of the modern service economy grow through the ruins of an industrial society. And with them emerges a sense of the things that history can bring to people that the heritage industry can tend to obscure: difference, displacement, and a questioning of our ordinary, mortal lives. What will become of us in the future?

England is full of ghosts. They constitute an absence which defines us. In the three decades after the Second World War the English imagined themselves a natural given, like the rolling green of the South or the bleak moors of the north, sustaining themselves with visions of a warrior nation of virtue, endurance and physical courage. And yet for all this national myth-making there was a dissonance in its telling. We were living through the final years of the long, stubborn demise of the late Victorian imperial age, a Teutonic nation of class deference shuddering to an ignominious end with the birth of youth culture, modern consumerism and New Commonwealth immigration. Even today this martial, status-obsessed world erupts into public view with a royal funeral, or the anniversary of a military event, the archaic symbols of royalty and tradition reinvigorating a glorious myth of England. Gripped in this dreamlike version of the past, the English are very close to the ghosts we have inherited; those other dead which our heritage frequently evades confronting.

We have appeased these ghosts with legends about Alfred burning the cakes, the courage of Richard the Lionheart, the compassion of Florence Nightingale. The past has been depicted as a magical place, and history as a reverie in which the English can affirm our conservative soul. Its mythology has shaped how we think about ourselves and who we think we are, both the horizon and the background of our everyday experience. The promotion of a national heritage connects our consciousness of our individual pasts to a social past in which 'I' becomes the 'we' of a singular, ethnic national community. Its narratives, ideologies, metaphors and fantasies fuse together the present and past into an undifferentiated union. Heritage becomes the attempt to make sense of the social past without disturbing the social and symbolic order of the present.

In *The Birth to Presence* Jean-Luc Nancy describes the task of making sense as 'death work'; and the work of mourning as an act of fending off the dead. It is, he argues, 'the very work of representation. In the end, the dead will be represented, thus held at bay.'[2] Heritage, in its attempts to bring the past back to life, epitomises this paradox. Symptomatic of a state of unresolved mourning, it represents a loss that cannot be accepted and must be continually returned to, even as it is denied.

John Everett Millais's painting The Boyhood of Raleigh (1870) hangs in Tate Britain, the museum dedicated to the history of British art. The painting is a precursor to the heritage industry of the late twentieth century; a masculine, romanticised story of an empire built on virtue and idealism. In Millais's homage to the progenitor of Victorian imperialism, two small Elizabethan boys listen intently as a Genoese sailor, his finger pointing to the open sea, regales them with his stories of seafaring adventure. The young Walter Raleigh, his hands clasping his knees which are drawn up to his chest, does not look at the sailor, nor follow the man's pointing finger. Even as he listens, he is lost in his own thoughts, daydreaming of his own destiny. What holds the attention are Raleigh's eyes. Roland Barthes describes how images have 'punctums', the element of a picture which arrests our gaze, and which makes it meaningful and memorable. It is what the viewer adds to the image but which is nonetheless already there; a form of aesthetic communication which draws us into an emotional engagement with the image.[3] Raleigh's eyes are an invitation to identify with his earnest self reflection and recall our own memories of childhood daydreaming. The boy's destiny, Millais tells us, is also our destiny: England's destiny.

In a nearby room is John Singleton Copley's painting The Death of Major Peirson (1781), the chronicle of an event of tragic, youthful heroism which gained iconic status in Georgian England. Its raw depiction of the chaos and violence of battle contrasts sharply with Millais's pre-Raphaelite wistfulness. The French have invaded Jersey and its capital St Helier has fallen. The young Major Peirson rejects the surrender and leads a successful counter-attack. In the meleé of soldiers fighting in the small square he is killed, and as he swoons back into the arms of his brother officers, the centre of the canvas is dominated by a lone, black soldier firing his musket at the assailant. Where is the punctum in this picture? Two figures stand out. Who is the black protagonist, where has he come from and what is his history? And in the bottom right hand corner of the square is a frightened boy, the young Singleton Copley, witness to the event, being hurried away by his fraught mother and nurse. Unlike Millais's romantic imperialism, Singleton Copley's picture is an act of remembrance which prompts us to ask questions about race, difference and history. It is a memory which allows an event in the past to become an object of thought.

Walter Benjamin, in his essay on his childhood 'A Berlin Chronicle', wrote that 'memory is not an instrument for exploring the past but its theatre. It is the medium of past experience, as the ground is the medium in which dead cities lie interred.'[4] He describes a discovery of the socially significant past which comes about not in an excavation of archives and texts, but through the archaeology of one's own self, in the relationship between actual events and cultural texts and the daydreams and fantasies evoked by them. Benjamin advises us to approach our buried pasts 'like a man digging', and not to be afraid to return again and again to the same matter. It is a past which is like an absence in the present. As André Green describes it, absence is an intermediary situation between presence and loss; it is something which is felt but its exact nature remains unknown.[5] It awaits meaning, and in this sense it represents the future. Benjamin's essay poses the past as a question. Dominant discourses and practices of heritage, in their attempt to bring the past into present life, can end up achieving the opposite effect. Past and present are fused together, and neither can be separated out or understood. What might come into being in the process of undoing this union? What would it reveal about who the English are, the nature of our individual selves?

Then

A good place to begin this investigation of subjectivity, and to trace its relationship to ideas about the past and heritage, is the late seventeenth century. It is the historical period which began to give form to the contours of our contemporary world: the 'possessive individualism' of commerce and trade capitalism; the cultural differences of femininity and masculinity; the emergence of colonialism and empires; the conflict between reason and feelings, commerce and sensibility; the divide between the public and private spheres of life; the making of the modern self. With the emergence of science and a metropolitan public culture over the following century, there occurred the secular development of the individual's inner life. The idea of reason began to challenge the parameters of ecclesiastical tradition. The religious ethic of righteousness was gradually surpassed by a pragmatism and psychology of the self. The Puritan's anxiety 'how can I be good?' became the secular 'how can I be happy?' At the same time, seventeenth-century maritime exploration and the colonial settlements which followed established a new understanding of the world which was central to the imagining of empire and empire making. The birth of modernity is characterised by this new spatial, geographical conception, and by the beginning of a language of the inner, psychological processes of the individual. Both are central to the modern articulation of identity and difference.

Daniel Defoe's *Robinson Crusoe*, published in 1719, arguably the first novel of modern England, offers a representation of this development. Historically located between the era of exploration and the birth of British colonialism, Crusoe is part missionary, part conquistador, part trader, part colonial administrator. 'September 30, 1659. I, poor miserable Robinson Crusoe, being shipwrecked, during a dreadful storm, in the offing, came on shore on this dismal unfortunate island, which I called the Island of Despair, all the rest of the ship's company being drowned, and myself almost dead.'[6] Shipwrecked on a slaving expedition to Africa, Robinson Crusoe begins his recollections in the diary he keeps on his castaway island. His despair is overcome by an extraordinary economic activity which transforms the uninhabited island into his 'little kingdom'. Crusoe's work orders time and space; 'Nov, 4th. This morning I began to order my times of work, of going out with my gun, time of sleep, and time of diversion' (p88). He produces an astonishing array of products; his fortress home, his domesticated animals, candles, clay pots and plates, and after three years his field of barley and rice and earthen vessels for baking bread. Crusoe is a figure of an ascendant middle-class culture, preoccupied by commerce, whose principle of freedom lies in unfettered economic individualism. For such a middle-class culture, the ideal free man is the man unconstrained by social relations.

The story of Robinson Crusoe lies on the threshold of modernity and marks a break with what Michel Foucault, in *The Order of Things*, calls the

Classical Age. Crusoe tells us early on in the story that he leaves his family for the adventures of seafaring because he wants to evade the calling of Providence. His adventure is an allegory for the birth of 'the West' and the social category of Man. The idea of the individual becomes the subject of language and representation.

> No doubt modernity begins when the human being begins to exist within his organism, inside the shell of his head, inside the armature of his limbs, and in the whole structure of his physiology; when he begins to exist at the centre of a labour by whose principles he is governed and whose product eludes him ... modern man – that man assignable in his corporeal, labouring and speaking existence – is only possible as a figuration of finitude.[7]

While the Classical Age was able to allot human beings a privileged position in the order of the world, Man could not appear as a subject of knowledge. In representation and language he is without boundaries or finitude. Crusoe tears himself free of this undifferentiated state in order to possess himself and secure an identity. He experiences his aloneness, and in his abandonment of Providential fate he is confronted with his finitude. This coming into being as an individual sets up a temporal and spatial polarity between now and then, presence and absence, self and other. Foucault writes that, 'The profound vocation of Classical language has always been to create a table – a "picture"'.[8] This is the space of representation that the category of Man destroys with his newly acquired form of knowledge or episteme. He brings himself into being through narrative, the advance of time, the recognition of his finitude, the knowledge of his death and the destruction of the old order.

On the island, Crusoe reflects on his lack of company, but dismisses the value of other men. His aloneness leads him to reflect on the benefits of his isolation. He has nothing to covet, nobody to lust after. Crusoe's island is one of intense privacy, a masculine idyll in which women are entirely absent. Emotion is subordinated to rational discourse. Scientific observations and the classification of experience distance him from compromising feelings. Everything Crusoe was capable of enjoying he has made himself, for himself alone; 'I was lord of the whole manor ... I might call myself king or emperor over the whole country which I had possession of' (p139). There are no rivals, no competition, nobody to dispute his omnipotence. But the movement which has created this isolated, utopian self-sufficiency, promises its destruction: 'Time – the time that he himself is – cuts him off not only from the dawn from which he sprang but also from that other dawn promised him as still to come.'[9] In his liminality and finitude, uprooted and adrift, Man is confronted with difference and what is Other to himself. Time, and with it experience, passes, and neither can be recovered.

The category of Man is founded on his capacity to think and the knowledge he establishes of and about himself. But this episteme does not affirm his being, rather it suggests a further binary of thought and the unthought: 'What must I be, I who think and who am my thought, in order to be what I do not think, in order for my thoughts to be what I am.'[10] Descartes's seminal 'I think therefore I am' is split. It can no longer guarantee the individual self, but plagues Man with self-doubt. Between the 'I think' and the 'I am', between the cogito and being, lies Man's unthought. It is this unknown which perpetually summons the individual toward self-knowledge, but thought alone cannot any longer think itself. It is not possible for Man to describe himself, without thought at the same time 'discovering, both in itself and outside itself, at its borders yet also in the very warp and woof, an element of darkness ... an unthought which it contains entirely, yet in which it is also caught.'[11] The category of Man is established in a confrontation with difference, in time passing and in the loss of experience.

Robinson Crusoe is an allegory of a European colonialism whose history has been Man's attempt to overcome difference. Everything which has established Crusoe's sovereignty, what he imagines to be his ontology, hewed from one foundation, is divided. 'It happened one day about noon going towards my boat, I was exceedingly suprized with the print of a man's naked foot on the shore, which was very plain to be seen in the sand.' After fifteen years, Crusoe's kingdom is shattered by the discovery of what does not belong to him. He hurriedly builds extra fortifications, all the while fearful of the threat from the 'out-side of my outer Wall'. So begins the years of primordial fear, of living in dread of being captured by savages and eaten. Crusoe's confrontation with the Other marks the end of his innocence. Its foreignness confirms, in his own mind, his identity and legitimate authority, but at the same time it signifies the unthought which divides him from himself. For Foucault, 'Man and the unthought are, at the archaeological level, contemporaries.'[12] The Other is born beside Man in an 'unavoidable duality', 'both exterior to him and indispensable to him … the shadow cast by man as he emerged in the field of knowledge … the blind stain by which it is possible to know him.'[13] In recognising both the interior and exterior of the unthought, what he imagines himself to be is no longer possible without the erasure of this threatening Other. For weeks afterwards, Crusoe's mind is filled with a desire for revenge. He sleeps fitfully, dreams of the pleasures of murder and suffers lurid nightmares. War must be declared, both within himself for mastery of his fear and against others for the threat they pose to his existence; either he devours or he will be devoured.

The purpose of such a war is to modify the spaces of the Other and incorporate them into the self. Its purpose is to collapse difference into sameness, to banish the unthought and once more fuse together 'I think' and 'I am' and recover the illusion of an homogeneous, internally undifferentiated individual. Man must become master of himself and of all that he sees. But this defensive strategy is impossible to fulfil because it undermines the preconditions of his existence. It is fuelled by a primordial desire to recapture the past and return to a state of non-differentiation with the world. The birth of 'the West' and its colonialism was not simply the assertion of economic and racial supremacy. The confrontation with difference precipitated a war of conquest to sustain Man's viability against the Other.

After twenty-four years alone on his island and nine years under the threatening shadow of the Other, Crusoe rescues Friday from ritualistic death and summons the era of the monologic, colonial imaginary:

I smiled at him, and looked pleasantly, and beckoned to him to come still nearer; at length he came close to me, and then he kneeled down again, kissed the ground, and laid his head upon the ground, and taking me by the foot, set my foot upon his head; this it seems was in token of swearing to be my slave for ever; I took him up, and made much of him, and encouraged him all I could (p207).

Not only does Crusoe rescue Friday from his own culture, he saves him from his own debased desire to be enslaved. In Friday's gratitude and Crusoe's benevolence the transgressive nature of Otherness is wiped away and the dominion of Man is confirmed. It is the relationship of the colonist to the native, the missionary to the convert and Man to his Other. Friday is incorporated into the colonial imaginary as the shadow of Crusoe's being, not a threatening unknown but a mimicry. Crusoe teaches Friday English – 'I ... taught him to say Master' – and, like his parrot, Friday's language is a debased simulacrum of Crusoe's own imperial identity: 'Yes, master' to Crusoe's 'No, Friday'. After all the threat and the terror, there is nothing to fear. The colonialist may now rule his territories as if they are uninhabited. On having to take notice of anyone, he will see only himself. Anything else is simply timeless and ghost like.

For Foucault the project of the episteme of Man is bound to fail. The Other, what is unthought, is larger than Man or his history and will expose the 'hollowness of our existence'.[14] Confronted with his own apocalyptic vision, Foucault can only ask himself a series of rhetorical questions about the nature of the modern episteme and the form of thought which might come after it. His response to this question is that, while he has no answers as to the future of European subjectivity, the significant fact is that he is able to ask these questions about its contemporary nature. 'I now know why I am able, like everyone else, to ask them – and I am unable not to ask them today.'[15] Foucault makes us question ourselves and our relationship to the Other, to time past and time present. But what do we do when we have asked the questions? There is an absolutism in his work that undermines the possibilities of ordinary human agency. For Foucault the unthought has the characteristic of being an inevitable and overwhelming force of negation which flattens temporality into space, turns history into geography and disintegrates the meaning and integrity of the individual self.

A more pragmatic response to the idea of the unthought is that it constitutes an absence which is filled with potential meaning. Just as it is the place
in which the subjectivity of Man is threatened, so it is also where new
subjectivities might emerge. The problems associated with the episteme of
Western individualism can be recognised and challenged without surren-
dering its positive achievements. Jean-Luc Nancy writes that 'whoever
comes after the subject, whoever succeeds to the West' will be a coming into
presence. 'Presence is what is born, and does not cease being born.'
Subjectivities are always 'in the midst of taking place'.[16] The Manichean
world of Robinson Crusoe originates in his fear of this indeterminacy,
projected out onto foreign lands and peoples different from himself. In
Defoe's fiction Crusoe's supremacy over Friday is conclusive. It is a desire to
fix identity and make it incommensurable to others. Its modern subjectivity attempts to 'master' the past, a relationship borne out of colonialism and
capitalist modernity.

However, even the most emphatic, monologic commentaries on race
and cultural identity contain their ambiguities. The most conservative
forms of heritage reveal the fault lines of their instabilities. An example of
this is the work of Rudyard Kipling. Two hundred years after the fictional
trials of Crusoe's early colonialism, Kipling's clarion call of imperialism is
not the unambiguous voice it at first appears to be. In his writing we can
recognise the contradictions and doubts of our own modern English identities.

Here and then

In 1902 Rudyard Kipling moved to his house 'Batemans' in Sussex and wrote
to an American friend, C. E. Norton. 'Then we discovered England which we
had never done before ... and went to live in it. England is a wonderful land.
It is the most marvellous of all foreign countries that I have ever been in. It
is made up of trees and green fields and mud and the gentry, and at last I'm
one of the gentry.' Kipling in many ways personifies the culmination of

Defoe's nascent imperial Man. He is remembered for his bellicose, barrack-room jingoism, and his promotion of the empire and its pageantry. But the truth is more complex. He was an Indian-born Englishman who became an immigrant in his native land and a foreigner in his own home. He belonged in neither one place nor another. Kipling lived at Batemans until his death in 1936, but he remained an odd man out and never quite made it into the ranks of the gentry. Unlike the fictional Crusoe he never succeeded in defeating the difference which haunted him.

In 1906 he published *Puck of Pook's Hill,* a book of stories which was an attempt to make himself feel at home in the Sussex landscape of Batemans.[17] The stories intertwine a heritage of the English with the lives and the future of his own two children:

> Land of our Birth, we pledge to thee
> Our love and toil in the years to be;
> When we are grown and take our place
> As men and women with our race

The central figure of the book is Puck, the Gate Keeper of Old England. Kipling uses him to introduce the children to men and women from England's past. He writes about heroism, moral courage, warriors, journeys, frontiers, explorations and the establishment of overseas territories. But rather than symbolising adventure and escape to foreign parts, the narratives are interred in the locality the children belong to, and seek to establish their relationship to the land. The book is a romanticised, sometimes sentimental version of history, but, despite this, Kipling does not offer his children a celebration of a familiar heritage.

The final tale of the book 'The Treasure and the Law' is about Kadmiel, a Jewish wanderer living in the early Middle Ages. Kipling's mythical vision of England is confronted by European modernity's symbolic figure of difference. The Jew is the stranger who is everywhere out of place. The story reveals Kipling's ambivalence about his own belonging. A frisson of uncertainty and doubt starts to unravel the fabric of the heritage he has taught his children.

'The Treasure and the Law' begins with Kadmiel's birth and the foretelling that he would be 'a Lawgiver to a People of a strange speech and hard language' (p228). Kadmiel sails to England to work for his uncle. The country is in a state of turmoil. The barons are fighting King John, borrowing money from Kadmiel's uncle to finance their war. When the barons attempt to secure another loan, Kadmiel demands that the barons amend the fortieth law of the Magna Carta which declares that 'to no free man will we sell, refuse or deny right of justice'. Kadmiel insists the words 'no free man' are replaced by the word 'none'. His demand is agreed, but then Kadmiel discovers that his uncle is planning to loan King John a secret hoard of gold which will enable him to raise an army and defeat the barons. The treasure has been hidden at the bottom of a tide-well in Pevensey Castle. In order to recover it, Kadmiel dives repeatedly into the tide-well, loads it into a boat, sails out into the English Channel and drops the treasure overboard. Kadmiel saves England from further war and ensures that 'there is but one Law in Old England for Jew or Christian' (p228).

Kipling gives no hint in the story that such tide wells were used as privies and that Kadmiel would have been forced to dive into 'Christian smelling' sewage. In a further twist to the plot, the gold originally belonged to two knights, Sir Richard and Sir Hugh, who, in a previous story in the book, had sailed to Africa where they had acquired it in exchange for worthless trinkets. 'Well,' said Puck calmly, concluding the story of Kadmiel ' ... the Treasure gave the Law. It's as natural as an oak growing' (p239). But the story is not 'natural'. Nothing is clear. *Puck of Pook's Hill* had appeared to be an unambiguous and seamless history of Old England. But by its end it is riven with ambiguities. Puck's statement is full of unconscious irony. African gold, discovered hidden beneath English shit, contributes to the development of an egalitarian English law. A Jew is the creator of free-born Englishmen. The treasure does not give the Law, but must be given up in order for there to be the Law. Loss establishes meaning. What is considered to be the same is created out of difference. What is foreign is the source of what is familiar.

What paternal lesson was Kipling imparting to his children in this final story? Perhaps he was unclear himself about his intentions. Tolerance of difference? A reflection of his own indeterminate status? Or a belief that the antithesis of ourselves is not to be feared but can be a source of renewal. These are radical and democratic sentiments one would not expect from a conservative imperialist. They might have taken root in his boyhood when he endured the misery of childhood exile from his home and family in an English prep school.[18] His holidays were spent in a foster home he called 'the House of Desolation' where his 'terrors' precipitated a nervous breakdown.[19] He could not endure his loss of his home and mother. It was a trauma that would not wear away into the past, but instead seized him in present time and evaded his understanding. He was a man who could never quite put the past behind him. Kipling was a patriot, but he was also a product of colonialism. He shared with Kadmiel the experience of being a man between places who was never sure of his identity. His story teaches us that what appears to be familiar always contains the seed of its own strangeness. We are never altogether what we imagine ourselves to be.

Now

Like the Styx which must be crossed to reach the underworld, the past is viewed as a boundary between the living and the dead, presence and absence. Heritage becomes an effort to mitigate its disruptive power, not so much by expelling it, but by attempting to incorporate it into the present. In the eighteenth century, prints of ruined castles and abbeys had a popular market. They provided the opportunity to reflect on transience and loss. Ruins were depicted as places of solitude and contemplation which could bring about a change in being. As Geoff Dyer remarks, '[r]uins don't make you think of the past, they direct you towards the future. The effect is almost prophetic. This is what the future will end up like. This is what the future has always ended up looking like.'[20] Ruins are only ruins if history passes them by and they are given up to the vagaries of time. Today, representations, artefacts and edifices of the past are integrated into the media, heritage and leisure industries in the form of reconstructions, tourism and pageantry. What matters is their recovery and preservation. To allow them to rot and fade back into the earth would be considered a transgression against a national culture. But their commodification encourages the idea of a perpetual present in which the past becomes a simulacrum. As a culture it becomes difficult to experience the loss of the past. Modern consumerism collapses the past into the present, death into life. Post-war Englishness has been informed by a mixture of nostalgia and bereavement. We have ended up wanting something that never goes away.

The heritage industry is shaped by this relationship to the past. It manufactures ghosts; the dead who cannot settle and remain caught in limbo neither fully present nor absent, prowling in the hope of release. As Freud noted, we unconsciously invent ghosts because of our sense of guilt in relation to the dead. They are the 'evil demons that have to be dreaded.'[21] Our dread comes from our fear of their retribution. It is only in the process of mourning that this fear of ghosts will diminish. When mourning has 'renounced everything that has been lost, then it has consumed itself, and our libido is once more free'.[22] In other words we have to remember before forgetting. Such a release transforms our relationship to the past. 'The same spirits who to begin with were feared as demons [are now] revered as ancestors and appeals are made to them for help.'[23]

Released from the grip of the past, how might we think historically in a way which helps us to face the future? I don't have an answer, but I have the idea that Freud's 'dreaming in broad daylight' might help me think about it. Imagine if Kipling, the estranged son who wrote the 'Treasure and the Law', sat down in the same room as the anti-colonial revolutionary Frantz Fanon. He would have been meeting his nemesis, the personification of everything his imperialism feared and hated. We could imagine him stepping into H.G. Wells' fictional time machine and taking a short trip into the future to see what had become of the imperialist world after the Second World War. The machine would have landed him in its heart, in Washington, USA in December 1961. Here he would have found Fanon bedridden with leukaemia. Fanon was thirty-six years old and in the last days of his life. He had come to America for medical treatment and found himself marooned and isolated in a strange country. His fame, which would sweep through the national liberation movements of the Third World, was still to come.

Picture the short, dapper Kipling with his Edwardian reserve sitting rather formally by the bedside of this infamous, once elegant black man. Fanon, who fought in the Algerian war of independence against France in the 1950s, was committed to destroying everything that Kipling had once championed. European humanism, he declared, had eulogised on the Rights of Man and yet 'murders men everywhere'.[24] Colonialism was the systematic negation of the other person, a furious determination to deny them all attributes of humanity. The people it subjugated were robbed of their identities and must, even now, constantly ask themselves: 'In reality, who am I?'[25] Fanon had spent his life seeking an answer to this question. He was a man who embodied Nancy's successor to the West and the philosophy of the Other coming into presence. The bloody and terrible affair of the successor that the 'West always demands, and always forecloses'.[26]

Despite Kipling's antipathy, Fanon's sad plight might have reminded him of his own beloved son John who was killed on the Somme, and whose death brought his trumpeting regard for English imperial bravado to an abrupt end. In this loss, Kipling might have recognised the common traits both men shared, not just the loneliness of dying, but a history of European colonialism which had united them in their difference. And with this in mind he might have found the opening gambit of a conversation: 'In our difference what might we hold in common...?'

NOTES

1. Cees Nootebum, *All Soul's Day*, Picador 2002, p167.

2. Jean-Luc Nancy, *The Birth to Presence*, Stanford University Press 1993, p3.

3. Roland Barthes, *Camera Lucida*, Flamingo 1982, p27.

4. Walter Benjamin, 'A Berlin Chronicle', in *One Way Street and Other Writings*, Verso 1985, p314.

5. André Green, 'The Analyst, Symbolization and Absence', *On Private Madness*, Hogarth Press 1986, p50.

6. Daniel Defoe, *Robinson Crusoe*, Penguin 1986, p89.

7. Michel Foucault, *The Order of Things: An Archaeology of the Human Sciences*, Routledge 1986, p318.

8. Ibid, p311.

9. Ibid, p335.

10. Ibid, p325.

11. Ibid, p326

12. Ibid.

13. Ibid.

14. Ibid, p375.

15. Ibid, p307.

16. Jean-Luc Nancy, op cit, p2.

17. Rudyard Kipling, *Puck of Pook's Hill*, Penguin 1995.

18. Rudyard Kipling, *Something of Myself*, Canto 1991, p5.

19. Ibid, p12.

20. Geoff Dyer, *Yoga For People Who Can't Be Bothered to Do It*, Abacus 2003, p204.

21. Sigmund Freud [1915], 'Our Attitude Toward Death', *Freud Pelican Library 12*, Penguin 1985, p82.

22. Sigmund Freud [1916], 'On Transience', *The Standard Edition of the Complete Works of Sigmund Freud*, Vol. XIV, Hogarth Press 1975, p307.

23. Sigmund Freud [1912-13], 'Totem and Taboo', *Freud Pelican Library 13*, Penguin 1990, p122.

24. Frantz Fanon, *The Wretched of the Earth*, Penguin 1990, p200.

25. Ibid.

26. Jean-Luc Nancy, op cit, p2.

three | Fallen among thieves

"Ours is a time when thieves are running after the robbed, screaming 'Oh! catch the thief'."

Mohsen Makhmalbaf

Sometimes on my way to work, when catching the tube to travel north and out of the city, I find myself standing close by two women sitting on one of the platform benches. One is elderly, the other younger, perhaps they are mother and daughter. They both look as if they have just walked from a North African souk, as, surrounding their feet and piled on the bench, their meagre possessions bulge out of plastic carrier bags. Their silent presence impels a series of questions. Who are they? Where are they from? What are they doing sitting here, huddling together dozing or staring nowhere in particular at 7.45am in the morning? Their strangeness and out-of-placeness, even in this neighbourhood of many ethnicities, provokes curiosity. In much the same way, several years earlier, when Roma women began working the area – begging with a characteristic robust determination and without a hint of servility – they prompted a mixture of fascination and, from some, outrage. In spite of the local cosmopolitan culture, the Roma exuded foreignness, and disrupted the settled coexistence of differences.

I live in a street where my neighbours' families have originated from Africa, Ireland, the Caribbean, the United States, Malta, Scotland, Mauritius, India. First, second or third generation, Hindu, Muslim,

Catholic, Protestant, Baptist, Sikh, we are here less because our individual choices have dictated it, and more because we are the products of historic migrations both within the British Isles and across the old Empire. The search for work and a better life, or forcible expulsion, has brought us from the Celtic nations to the South of England, from former colonies to the mother country. We are a neighbourhood of different communities, some with networks extending only to the next street, others which stretch across the world. It is a neighbourhood of porous boundaries in which it is difficult to identify who belongs and who is an outsider. What is it we belong to in this locality? What is it that each of us calls home and, when we think back and remember how we arrived here, what stories do we share? This is not the homogenous white culture of a middle England shire where inhabitants can trace their names back to the Domesday Book. The populating and depopulating of this street is symptomatic of the transience and historical discontinuities created by modernity. And yet the other week J, who lives across the road, said, 'I don't want any refugees here. We've got enough. I just don't want to know.' At that time, to the best of my reckoning, we had none. J is not someone who believes herself to be a racist – her children are mixed race – rather she believed that asylum seekers were a threat to her livelihood.

Welcome to England

Refugees, asylum seekers, economic migrants, are harbingers of a troubled world. By their nature they are unsettled; they remind us by their very presence of change and disruption. Many carry in their bodies and in their life stories the intimations of horror. They transport the bad news from a far corner of the world onto our doorsteps. They need resources and they need help and so invite envy, rage and suspicion. And yet for all their strangeness, if we who are settled are willing to look, we will recognise in them something familiar to our own lives. Asylum seekers symbolise the paradox of modernity – the historic opportunity to make a life for one's self, but at the same time the experiencing, in the promise of a better future, of a fearful sense of a loss of security, familiarity, home. We need not have experienced real homelessness and exile to feel the displacement and disorientation which pervades modern life. It was in the histories of grandparents and parents, who migrated from towns and villages to the city. It is in our own move from one house to the next, from one job to another. It is in our struggle to make an identity for ourselves and to negotiate the difficult transition into adulthood. Changes in lifestyle and mobility have also dislocated our sense of class belonging. The institutional support of marriage and the organisation of the extended family, which once structured and contained personal relationships, no longer holds sway. Religious and moral certainties have been questioned or rejected and we are increasingly thrown back onto our own personal resources and ethics. Our search for a more authentic, self-fulfilling way of life exposes us to what can become an anchorless, lonely and ephemeral existence, laden with personal risk.

Modernity – the historical experience of industrialisation, commercialism, modernisation and mass democracy – transformed the habitats of people from small, restrictive and conforming collectivities into the expansive, unpredictable flux of city life. This historical development has enhanced our individuality, and the opportunities for self-expression and realisation. Freedom from restrictive moralities and the confinements of a narrow communalism has created cultures in which being different and distinguishing ourselves from others have positive, aspirational meanings. But the cost has been the erosion of community and tradition.

At the beginning of the twentieth century, Georg Simmel was describing how the impact of modernity on individuals led to inner feelings of security being superseded by 'a faint sense of tension and vague longing', a 'secret restlessness' and a 'helpless urgency'.[1] It was Simmel who wrote about the stranger as the harbinger of these disruptive forces. Unlike the wanderer of an earlier time, who 'comes today and goes tomorrow', the stranger 'comes today and stays tomorrow'.[2] The asylum seeker is the modern day stranger, a portent of the destructive, liberating, frightening, cruel, exhilarating powers of modernity. The loss of a previous way of life personified in the asylum seeker echoes our own experience of loss. You can never fully experience being at home, nor find your way back to what you imagine home had been. Home becomes an idealised memory, longed for but impossible to recover.

This essay isn't about asylum seekers. Asylum seekers do not imagine themselves to be the portent of anything other than their own desperate quest for life. It is about those of us who have settled and who find strangers at our gate, who feel trepidation at the thought of our localities being disrupted, and what is familiar to us being despoiled. It is about the large numbers who read newspapers like the *Daily Mail* and are susceptible to their daily outpouring of xenophobia and twisted fabrications about asylum seekers. In the last two decades the decline of welfare provision, the deregu-lated jobs market, increasing inequality, fear of debt, crime, unemployment and isolation have intensified our pursuit of individual security. The idea that 'we're all in it together' has been superseded by the belief that survival and getting on is down to 'me alone'. We live in a society where the value of trust has been diminished. The promotion of individualised rational choice as a way of governing and regulating the population has encouraged a retreat into private life and the 'privatisation' of happiness. Values of solidar-ity and civic obligation have been dissipated, and their demise encourages a culture of self-interest and paranoia. Disquiet at the quality of contempo-rary public life leads to a nostalgia for an idealised home and community. Zygmunt Bauman describes this nostalgia as the dream of 'defensible space': 'a place with secure and effectively guarded borders, a territory semantical-ly transparent and semiotically legible, a site cleansed of risk, and particu-larly of the incalculable risks – which transform merely "unfamiliar people" … into downright enemies'.[3]

The fantasy of this privatised home of order, security and predictability finds its collective expression in a mythical historical community. For white England it is a belief in its own timeless continuity of freeborn people and the rule of law. The former Conservative Prime Minister John Major described this English idyll as 'the country of long shadows on county grounds, warm beer, invincible green suburbs, dog lovers and pool fillers and – as George Orwell said "old maids cycling to Holy Communion through the morning mist"'.[4] This is a pastoral myth, central to understanding how England has been represented historically: a country which believes in 'order and tradition': 'romantic, illogical, muddled, divinely lucky, Anglican, aristocratic, traditional, frivolous'.[5] But the sentimentality obscures a domestic streak of paranoia. Thus the *Daily Mail* sounded the alarm on 6 September 2003: 'They're Back. The new asylum army massing in Calais' ... 'They stand in a bedraggled queue waiting for food handouts ... massing in numbers readying for a renewed invasion of Britain'.

The politics of xenophobia and anti immigration is fuelled by a rhetoric about numbers, and legitimised by the pseudo scientific use of statistics: the level of birth rates amongst ethnic minorities; how many immigrants entered the country this year compared to last year; the projected populations of ethnic minorities in twenty, fifty, one hundred years time; the growing numbers demanding housing, health and social services. A melange of statistics claiming scientific objectivity reduces asylum seekers to a threatening, homogenous mass. The contemporary representation of the asylum seeker as a foreign parasite overwhelming its host culture recalls earlier reaction to twentieth-century immigration. 'There is no end to them in Whitechapel and Mile End. It is Jerusalem', complained undertaker William Walker of the Jewish immigrants in 1903. 'If they once get any power, they will multiply, and we will be snowed under by them', warned a Bradford resident of New Commonwealth immigrants in 1964.[6] Enoch Powell, in his infamous 1968 Rivers of Blood speech, revealed even more desperation:

> It almost passes belief that at this moment twenty or thirty additional immigrant children are arriving from overseas in Wolverhampton alone every week – and that means fifteen or twenty additional families a decade or two hence. It is like watching a nation busily engaged in heaping up its own funeral pyre.[7]

Like Powell, the tabloid press today alludes to 'facts and figures' to construct asylum seekers as the impending apocalypse. *The Daily Star* headline on 5 August 2003 was 'Tories: We are the TB capital of the world'. In fact Britain's rate of tuberculosis per 100,000 is 10.1 compared to the highest reported incidence of 142.6 per 100,000 in Cambodia. On 3 September 2003, the *Daily Mail* exclaimed: 'Britain still the world's asylum capital'. In fact Britain's refugee population at that time was under 160,000, as compared with Iran, which topped the league with 1.3 million.[8] The final paragraph of the *Daily Mail's* 6 September report illustrates the ploy of insinuating that official government statistics and hence the policies based on them are worthless: 'Although government figures show asylum seekers down by 34 per cent – from 16,000 a month early this year to 10,585 a month in the summer – critics say there is no evidence that the numbers coming to the country illegally have fallen.' The question of who these critics are and how they have been able to achieve this calculation is brushed aside by an appeal to populist prejudice. The subtext is straightforward: 'Whatever their facts claim, we KNOW we're being swamped'.

In March 2003 Home Secretary David Blunkett announced his proposals for appeasing the irrational and virulent opposition to asylum seekers. Regional protection zones would address the issue of asylum claims arising from regional conflicts or natural disasters. Transit zones would process asylum claims without people travelling to the countries in which they want to seek asylum.[9] These proposed measures, with their language of camps in which human rights would be suspended, prompt comparison with earlier attempts in Europe to eradicate racial difference within its populations. Stephen Byers, a New Labour ideologue and former Transport Secretary, explained the government's reasoning for these policies: 'It is clearly the case that many of Labour's traditional supporters are those that fear immigration the most. They are concerned that their schools and health services are under increased pressure, that in some way their national identity is under threat and that they have to pay for people who are simply exploiting the present system.'[10] Despite being progressive on a number of other social issues, New Labour, rather than launching a robust challenge to the widespread uninformed prejudice on this question, capitulated to the xenophobia. And its political timidity has served to encourage the emergence of an imaginary 'British homeland' that is parochial, culturally conservative and self absorbed: one, moreover, that has been privatised and left prone to fear and insecurity.

It is not easy to love one's neighbour as one's self, let alone a complete stranger. But refugees and those seeking a better life for themselves and their families call for an ethical response from the host society. Can we create a collective response to migration which is a mutual give and take, just and equal, and based on a concern for the other? This essay is about developing such an ethics of hospitality. It is about how we might fashion an idea of home which is not some absolute ontological root of our life, but an imaginary location in which we are able to live with ourselves and with others.

Such an ethical response to asylum seekers is shaped by material factors. It is easier to believe one's self to be liberal and tolerant when one is relatively well off and living in a secure neighbourhood, protected from interlopers by inflated house prices. It is much harder to be tolerant living on a beleaguered, impoverished estate after two generations of unemployment. In our unequal society, the indigenous poor and disinherited are more likely to feel themselves in competition for the resources distributed to asylum seekers. Our ethical response to others is not simply a private moral concern, it is about politics.

Paul Ricoeur argues that politics gives ethics a sphere in which to operate. Politics puts into continuing social existence a constitutive requirement of ethical intention – 'the requirement of mutual recognition – the requirement that makes me say: your freedom is equal to my own'.[11] Politics is the 'creation of spaces of freedom', whose rule is given legal form by the state. The idea of an ethics of hospitality means the freedom to give; its precondition must be a politics that creates freedom from want. In the first instance it means the commitment to inclusiveness and equality amongst the indigenous population. An ethics of hospitality requires the capacity of a society to manage and absorb the unpredictable and surprising. It has to possess the necessary resources to give something to strangers and not feel itself depleted – and this is not simply a question of ownership of goods and money, but one of belonging to a culture which many value and which

[handwritten margin notes: perhaps intolerance on this point stems from people feeling that they haven't been given to?]

values all. Hospitality enhances integrity and good in such a culture, because the burden of collective giving is transparently shared by all equally. And it is a reparative culture, in the sense that it promotes the value of social relations and builds institutions which have emotional intelligence. The act of giving is based on the experience of having been given to.

A new idea of home, an ethics of being with others, a more equal distribution of wealth and resources, a recognition of emotional life, are the constitutive requirements for an ethics of hospitality. But the enactment of these ethics requires an historical context. The negative response to asylum seekers amongst sections of the white English population has been influenced by a history of empire. Its imagery and vocabulary has been reproduced in countless films, adventure stories, newspaper reports and politician's speeches, giving shape to a racialised language of national community. The words used to denigrate asylum seekers belong to the social and linguistic fabric of the English ethnic culture we have inherited. Whatever the date – 1901, 1964, 1968, 2003 – the racial language of swamping, breeding, cheating, threatening, parasitical foreigners remains remarkably constant. In order to challenge this language and the paranoia it arouses, it is first necessary to understand its history.

Over there

The era of the New Imperialism of the 1890s, when European powers scrambled for Africa, gave rise to a chauvinistic arrogance amongst large sections of the British population. To be a white Englishman became the apotheosis of good standing. This belief remains a powerful contemporary myth in English nationalist sentiment. It has fuelled the self-justifications of English fascists and football hooligans, and informed the media representations of British troops in the second Iraq war – where their moral virtue and courage was compared favourably to that of their more unreliable, violence-prone US counterparts. The ubiquitous coverage of the SAS has similarly attempted to sustain the myth of a virtuous and hardy warrior nation. What remains unsaid is that this myth is still powerfully symbolised by white skin colour.

There is another less obvious but more complex history which has shaped responses to asylum seekers and which helps to explain not only the paranoia, but also the persistence of the historical myths of Englishness. I can best illustrate this with a minor event from a period before the heyday of Empire. In 1834, a young Englishman named Alexander Kinglake entered the gates of Belgrade.[12] He was twenty-five years old and had attended Cambridge University where he had read for the Bar. Like many of his kind who came before and after, Kinglake's eyes were set on 'the splendour and havoc of the East'. His travels took him across Asia Minor, and down through Syria to Gaza, a town which stood on the fringes of the desert. After negotiating with the Governor, and having gathered his supplies and purchased the use of four camels, Kinglake, his attendant Dthemetri, and the four Arab owners of the camels, set out for the ten-day journey to Cairo. The desert landscape was featureless: 'the hills and valleys are sand, sand, sand, still sand, and only sand, and sand, and sand again'. He looks to the sky for contrast but there is only the 'flaming sword of the sun'. No words are spoken, the only sight is the 'pattern and the web of the silk that veils your eyes, and the glare of the outer light'. Time labours on. Each night Kinglake walks out into the desert to experience the loneliness of its expanse. Standing in the nothingness, he is filled with a childish exultation. When he retraces his footsteps and arrives back at the small encampment with its glowing fire and the Arabs 'humming old songs about England' he feels as if he has arrived home.

Kinglake's response to the utter strangeness of the desert is to fabricate for himself the familiarity of home. What he sees in the small encampment is a poignant and intense idealisation of his own belonging. A similar response was registered by the adventure novelist John Buchan. In 1901, aged twenty-six, he had been recruited by Lord Milner, High Commissioner to South Africa, to serve in the South African Service. He wrote to his sister Anna about his arrival in South Africa. It was a country 'strange and new to the sight and yet familiar to the imagination. This was the old Africa of a boy's dream'.[13] Historical and fictional accounts of colonial encounters allude to this sense of familiarity, as if the foreign unknown had always already been known to the colonialist. Edward Ingram compares the predictability of this colonial culture with another significant Victorian representation, Alice's Wonderland:

> The foreign lands he travels in, the vile climate he endures, the natives he manages: all of them exist in a daydream exactly opposite to Alice's ... whereas Alice staggers in Wonderland from surprise, to astonishment, to crisis, as one by one everything – space, time, meaning, causation – she has taken for granted is denied her, the [colonial] reinforces the values and habits of the world he has supposedly left but to which he will assuredly return.[14]

As long as the natives are firmly controlled, or for reasons of their own make a show of obeisance, the colonialist may live in a daydream, his life stable owing to his confidence that his daydream will not be interrupted. When he surveys his dominions it is like looking in a mirror: he only ever sees the world he has conjured up within himself.

Psychoanalysis defines this kind of psychological response to others as projection. Freud describes projection as an internal perception which is unconsciously repressed: 'Its content, after undergoing a certain kind of distortion, enters consciousness in the form of an external perception.'[15] Intolerable feelings of, for example, greed, fear, or socially unacceptable sexual desires, are repressed and expelled out into the external world. They are projected into individuals and groups who are then identified as being greedy, persecutory or hypersexual. Intolerance towards inner, persecutory feelings is translated into an intolerance towards the individual or group who have been invested with their traits. The empire provided an ideal screen of colonised people for this kind of projection. It enabled an English identity to be affirmed through its difference to and rejection of other cultures. As André Green remarks: 'the foreign culture is loaded with all the evils against which the active culture defends itself ... The evil it refuses to recognise in itself, it denounces mercilessly in the other.'[16] This is what Edward Said was pointing towards when he described the psychological character of the West's attitude toward the East as 'a form of paranoia'.[17]

Subordinated cultures are perceived as primitive, dangerous, unpredictable, inferior, naive, and in need of looking after and controlling. The British imperialist imagined himself to be like a mother/father who knows his subjects. It is as if parts of his self had entered into the native population, where they resided and exerted control. This projection evoked in him feelings of omnipotence and benevolence. One District Commissioner of the Colonial Service explained his aspirations as he set out for Africa after the Second World War:

> Since my schooldays it had been my ambition to be a District Commissioner in the Colonial Service ... I wanted Power, but not pomp and ceremony. The Power that would enable me to show mercy, to redress wrongs, to dispense justice, and to lead and guide people toward a better, more prosperous and peaceful life.[18]

However idealistic and altruistic the British Imperial Mission imagined itself to be, there was the expectation that the white man's gift should be reciprocated by the loyalty, even gratitude, of the native. The realities of power, backed up by military and police violence, which were necessary to maintain this psychic economy of projection, were conveniently overlooked.

The daydream of empire depended upon the sanctity of the homeland. For centuries British Imperialism imposed its history onto other people's homelands, never contemplating a time when the movement of culture and identities might go into reverse. The loss of empire and the various waves of twentieth-century immigration to Britain – from the West Indies in the 1950s, India, Pakistan and East Africa in the 1960s, Eastern Europe, Somalia, and a range of other nationalities at the millennium – rudely awakened the English from their collective daydream. No longer able to project internal contradictions and conflicts out into foreign lands, England was confront-ed with what it had denied and repressed about itself. The benign sense of omnipotence and complacent belief in racial superiority was replaced by a strange half silence, half denial about the end of empire. Unable to project onto defenceless others, the dominating English culture experienced a weakening of its sense of identity. What does it mean to be English? With each wave of immigration, sections of the population exhibited a sense of vulnerability which expressed itself in bullying: they persecuted the incomers because they felt persecuted by them. The near-hysterical reaction to asylum seekers is a typical example of this collective paranoia. As David Bell describes:

> The 'asylum seeker' who claims to need protection from us is really 'on the make', seeing us as 'a soft touch'. If we allow them in, we will be opening our doors to a flood of greedy individuals who will take possession of our commonwealth and destroy 'our way of life'.[19]

Bell goes on to explain how this paranoid fantasy enables the denial of any feelings of guilt or responsibility for the predicament of asylum seekers. It follows a singular brutal narrative: 'Their plight is of their own making. We owe them NOTHING'.

In the face of this history we need to create a commonwealth of difference. This is a task that has been shrouded in a fog of denial and evasion, and one which mainstream British politics has been wary of addressing. An essay by David Goodhart, the editor of *Prospect*, which was subsequently published in *The Guardian*, illustrates the extent to which parts of the white, liberal intelligentsia, confronted by populist prejudice against asylum seekers, have retreated from this task.[20] Goodhart argues that the growing diversity of British society (by which he means ethnic diversity) is threatening to undermine its social cohesion and the values of solidarity which underpin the welfare state. Tellingly, his definition of the problem is borrowed from the Conservative politician David Willets:

> The basis on which you can extract large sums of money in tax and pay it out in benefits is that most people think that the recipients are people like themselves, facing difficulties that they themselves could face. If values become more diverse, if lifestyles become more differentiated, then it becomes more difficult to sustain the legitimacy of a universal risk-pooling welfare state. People ask: 'Why should I pay for them when they are doing things that I wouldn't do.'[21]

Goodhart does not reject this argument – like New Labour, he succumbs to it, thus enabling its ideology to define the debate about asylum seekers. Willets is disingenuous. The question he believes people will ask is one that the rich have repeatedly and insistently asked, throughout the history of the welfare state. The Conservatives gave them the answer they wanted in 1979, when Margaret Thatcher became Prime Minister, and threw into reverse the redistributive logic of the welfare state. That year, income tax on the top rate of earnings was reduced from 83 per cent to 60 per cent, and in 1988 it fell to 40 per cent.[22]

It is economic inequality, not ethnic differences, which is the main driver of social and cultural division. Goodhart, however, justifies his position by defining citizenship not as simply an abstract idea of rights and obligations, but as something that 'we' are born into. 'When politicians talk about the "British people" they refer ... to a group of people with a special commitment to one another.'[23] To sustain this argument of course, he must ignore a whole history of prejudices and inequalities internal to the 'British People': the differences between the Celtic countries and England, between regions, between Catholics and Protestants, between the classes, between men and women, and between the rich and the poor. The industrial revolution and enclosures of common land in the early nineteenth century, which gave shape to the British class system, were predicated on a profoundly divided society. The middle and upper classes perceived the masses of the poor as dangerous outsiders in a similar manner to the *Daily Mail's* representation of asylum seekers. They thus inflicted on them the brutalities of the workhouse and the penal system. Goodhart fails to acknowledge that the 'special commitment' that has sometimes managed to unite a national community against its own internal divisions has been the ideological appeal of race and nation. The romanticised image of an undivided 'we' colludes with the racial discourses which have historically shaped white English ethnicity in its antithesis to Catholics, Jews, Asians, Africans, indeed all who don't belong to its imagined community and pastoral landscape.

[margin note: Historical context]

For politics to enable an ethics of hospitality to develop it has to bring into question this idealised national community and the history that has given it shape. Its myth is the lifeblood of the xenophobe and its promise of belonging a harbour for the insecure. Hate has to be confronted, fear offered solace and an alternative – a process which addresses two sides of the same coin. Each of us is born with a past, and the stories of our lives are partly the stories of the communities from which we derive our identity. We are part of history and the bearers of a tradition, but as the philosopher Alasdair MacIntyre persuasively argues, we are not bound by their moral and political limitations.[24] Rather than allowing history and tradition to congeal us into an inert and deadened mindset, they can be resources for renewal and development: the places from which we begin. An ethics of hospitality cannot grow out of guilt or denial of the past. It requires that we find different ways of thinking about home and belonging, allowing our identities to change in our relationship to others.

The ethics of hospitality

When we first moved into our house, our neighbour was an old man who lived with his dog and never spoke a word to anyone. His dog died and he soon followed, lying at the foot of the stairs, down which he'd fallen. He had no family and his house was boarded up and soon became a refuge for drinkers and junkies, who over a period of several years fought, lit fires and yelled through the night as if they were enacting scenes from one of Pieter Bruegel's medieval nightmares. The very close proximity of these disturbances invaded our home, not simply with noise but also with an aura of fear. Then a distant cousin of the deceased owner saw quite by accident an advert in her local paper, claimed the property and sold it. Our new neighbours, the Ls, cleaned and repaired the house and moved in. Within two years they had left for more upmarket surroundings, renting out their property through an agency. A succession of refugee families moved in. Each would decamp more rapidly than the last, fleeing a steadily deteriorating building. No-one stayed. One year the house would be in deathly silence, the next it would be overcrowded and bursting with life. Over time it permeated the immediate locality with an atmosphere of transience and neglect. Then, after one resident and her children had done a midnight flit with half the furniture, the house was left open, exposing a pitiable, poverty-stricken slum. Living in its proximity for twenty years generated in our family a longing for someone permanent to move in and dispel the mood of decline and insecurity that inhabited the building. When the Ls finally gave up in despair and sold it, it was as if our own home had been re-admitted to the commonality of the neighbourhood. Reintegrated. Rendered secure. Made safe.

Poverty and deprivation generate social insecurity. In afflicted areas, neither the market nor an impoverished public sector can establish a common ground which mediates the relationship of individuals to the public world. Without this established common ground individuals have great difficulty in managing risk and absorbing change. They are abandoned to the social dislocations of poor housing and the unregulated markets of drugs, jobs and debt. The boundary between private life and the public world is tenuous and flimsy, driving people ever further into the illusory safety of their homes. The front door is no longer an opening onto the world but the gate of a besieged fortress whose walls have been irreparably breached. This is the reality of deprivation; and yet we find that the fear and paranoia associated with it has permeated swathes of the population where no tangible threat exists. However much we accumulate in the way of worldly goods, social insecurity is endemic in our mass, individualised society. Hannah Arendt suggests that such a society destroys both the public and private realms. People are deprived 'not only of their place in the world but of their private home, where they once felt sheltered against the world.'[25] The 'problem' created by asylum seekers in a rich industrialised nation like Britain is not related to a lack of material resources but to the deprivation of a common life. We live insecurely in the world to the degree that strangers create anxiety and hatred. Even the persecuted are shown little sympathy. Asylum seekers confront us with the need to recreate social interconnected-ness.

In his essay 'The Socius and the Neighbour', Paul Ricoeur points out that there is no sociology of the neighbour. However, it might be possible to create one, situated 'between a sociology of human relationships and a theology of charity'.[26] He begins with the parable of the Good Samaritan:

A certain man went down from Jerusalem to Jericho, and fell among thieves, who also stripped and wounded him ... And it happened that a priest went down the same way ... In like manner a Levite also passed by ... But a certain Samaritan being on his journey came near him; and seeing him, was moved with compassion ... Which of these three men, in thy opinion, was neighbour to him that fell among the thieves?[27]

Ricoeur notes that the two men who fail to stop and help the stricken man are defined by their social category of priest and Levite. He describes them as men absorbed in their social function. In them, the ecclesiastical institution bars their access to the encounter with the victim (p99). In contrast the Samaritan is a stranger 'impure in race and in piety', a non-category without a past or authentic traditions. In stopping he invents a conduct that is 'the direct relationship of "man to man"'. The Samaritan is a person through his capacity to encounter. His 'compassion' is a gesture 'over and above roles, personages, and functions' (p99-100). Ricoeur describes this as a hyper-sociological mutuality. He defines the neighbour as 'the personal way in which I encounter another, over and above all social mediation' (p101).

What does this kind of naked or bare encounter mean in our highly socially mediated society? And is the idea of an unmediated encounter anterior to social relations an illusion? Modern society is a world of mediated relationships which Ricoeur describes as the 'socius': the 'socius' is 'the person I attain through his social function' (p101). Who then is my neighbour? Ricoeur answers this question by asserting the false nature of the polarity between the neighbour and the 'socius'. They are in fact the two dimensions of the same history. He gives as an example his love for his own children, which does not exclude an active concern for the well being of all children: 'I am not discharged of all responsibility to other children by simply loving my own' (p103). Instead of polarising into opposites the bare life of the neighbour and the mediated world of the 'socius', Ricoeur argues that it is necessary to 'constantly seek out the unity of intention underlying the diversity of my relations to others. It is the same charity which gives meaning to the social institution and to the event of the encounter' (p103). The bare, face-to-face encounter with the neighbour cannot be separated from the social context which gives it its historical impact. There is a dialectic between the neighbour and the socius: 'At times the personal relationship to the neighbour passes through the relationship to the socius; sometimes it is elaborated on the fringes of it; and at other times it rises against the relationship of the socius' (p105).

For most of us, the kind of bare encounter described in the parable of the Samaritan is an infrequent event. Our encounters with suffering bodies are usually mediated by social institutions and by media representations. The object of charity usually appears 'only when I attain, in the other man, a common condition which takes on the form of a collective misfortune – colonial exploitation, racism' (p105). This fact poses a problem for Ricoeur. In an increasingly instrumentalised public world, it becomes harder to establish a relationship to the neighbour. Increasingly it can only occur in its interstices and on its margins. People turn away from the public realm to the 'warmth and intimacy of authentic personal exchanges and encounters' in the private realm. Modern society has tended to divide and oppose the neighbour and the 'socius' as belonging to the private and public. But Ricoeur is adamant that this is an evasion of reality: 'there is no private life unless it is protected by public order ... the social establishes the private' (p106). An instrumental, utilitarian public realm blocks access to the personal and hides 'the mystery of interhuman relationships' (p108). What is lacking in social existence, he says, is charity. The theme of the neighbour is 'an appeal to the awakening of consciousness' and a 'permanent critique of the social bond' (p108). But it is not a moral critique confined to personal relationships and private acts of charity. As Ricoeur points out, bourgeois charity can become an alibi for justice. Ricoeur concludes: 'we remain in history, that is, within the debate between the socius and the neighbour, without knowing whether charity is here or there' (p109).

Ricoeur offers little comfort in this contingent, uncertain practice of charity. It is political, but it lacks any coherent ideology. Its impulse originates in the mercy shown to human suffering which finds its substantive meaning in his own Christian ethics. The politics that has claimed to be the precondition and constitutive requirement for this act of giving has been socialism. Its ideology and practice, however, in its broad manifestation, has tended to displace the agency of personal ethics by promoting the mediating function of the state and social institutions. The desire to thwart the hypocrisies of bourgeois charity and to highlight the inadequacies of private giving has paradoxically weakened the impulse that gave it life. Today, the politics of social market managerialism practised by New Labour has been entirely emptied of an ethics of hospitality. Its approach to asylum seekers has been to marginalise humanitarian concern in favour of an instrumental argument favouring economically useful immigration and the rapid expulsion of non-useful human beings. Similarly, in schools, hospitals and social services, the ethic of care has been seriously eroded by the imposition of a market-based regime of cost benefit analysis and calculation. The social relationships which lie at the heart of teaching, health care and social work have been withered by the managerialist demand for audit, targets and measurement. In thinking how to articulate and put into practice an ethics of hospitality we are faced with public institutions that have been emotionally and democratically impoverished. The traditions of socialism and Christianity that have been the principal resources for sustaining a public life and establishing an ethics of giving have become marginal belief systems in contemporary consumer society.

In his book *Means Without End*, the philosopher Giorgio Agamben issues a challenge: 'The refugee should be considered for what it is, namely, nothing less than the limit-concept that at once brings a radical crisis to the principles of the nation state and clears the way for a renewal of categories that can no longer be delayed.'[28] He argues that the refugee as stranger and marginal figure is no longer representable inside the nation state and consequently 'unhinges the old trinity of state-nation-territory' (p22). The implications of this challenge were taken up by Jacques Derrida in his essay 'On Cosmopolitanism': 'How can the right to asylum be redefined and developed without repatriation and without naturalisation?'[29] His call for 'cities of refuge' draws on models of sanctuary founded in early Jewish law on the right of asylum. His proposal gives thought to Heidegger's homelessness of mortals which calls mortals into their dwelling (see chapter 2): 'I also imagine the experience of cities of refuge as giving rise to a place (lieu) for reflection – for reflection on the questions of asylum and hospitality – and for a new order of law and democracy to come to be put to the test' (p21).

Derrida's notion of 'cities of refuge' draws on the past to inject a new vigour into public life, and signal a future politics. His call is a response to a human predicament, and in his response a politics can be identified and given shape. An ethics of hospitality is not waiting to be discovered. It has to be made out of history, constituted by the political forces in existence, using the traditions of ethical life which are at hand. As Ricoeur states, 'one does not have a neighbour; I make myself someone's neighbour'.[30] It is a relationship that must be brought into existence both ethically, within me, in response to another's suffering, and politically, in the making of a common good. Creating the common good is a task central to democratic participation. Where does this process begin? Not with abstracted ideals or utopian visions of a perfect world. It begins in the contingency and unpredictability of the encounter with our neighbour. It takes shape in the disturbing, disorienting confrontation with our own fear of what this engagement will mean. In our neighbour we will see reflected the image they perceive of us. To the question 'who am I?' we will not necessarily get the answer we expect or would like. In this encounter an ethics is made. An ethics of hospitality is not a one-way street, but a mutual recognition of a common humanity, in which lies, for each of us to find, our individual integrity, a common life, the reason why we breathe.

NOTES

1. Georg Simmel, *Philosophy of Money*, trans. T. Bottomore and D. Frisby, Routledge 1978.
2. Georg Simmel, 'The Stranger', in *On Individuality and Social Forms*, ed. Donald Levine, University of Chicago Press 1971, p143.
3. Zygmunt Bauman, 'The Stranger Revisited – and Revisiting', in *Life in Fragments: Essays in Postmodern Morality*, Blackwell 1995, p135.
4. John Major, House of Commons, 22 April 1993. I was reminded of this speech by Timothy Garton Ash in 'The Janus dilemma', *Guardian*, 5.6.04.

5. Martin J. Weiner, *English Culture and the Decline of the Industrial Spirit 1850-1980*, Penguin 1981, p42.

6. Quotes taken from John A. Garrard, 'Parallels of Protest: English Reactions to Jewish and Commonwealth Immigration', *Race* Vol. IX, No.1, July 1967.

7. See Humphrey Berkeley, *The Odyssey of Enoch: A political memoir*, Hamish Hamilton 1977, pp129-137.

8. Examples taken from *Update* newsletter for supporters of the refugee council, December 2003.

9. David Blunkett – see Home Office press release, 27.3.03.

10. Stephen Byers, 'Speech on asylum and immigration to the Social Market Foundation', 30.7.03, http://society.guardian.co.uk/asylumseekers/story/0,7991, 1009688,00.html

11. Paul Ricoeur, 'Ethics and Politics', in *From Text to Action*, Trans. Kathleen Blanney, John B. Thompson, Athlone Press, London 1991, p332.

12. His account of his journey, *Eothen*, published in 1844, made him a much sought-after figure in literary London. For quotes, see A.W. Kinglake, *Eothen*, Longmans, Green and Co 1935.

13. Janet Adam Smith, *John Buchan: A Biography*, Oxford 1985, p131.

14. Edward Ingram, 'The *Raj* as Daydream: the Pukka Sahib as Henty Hero in Simla, Chandrapore, and Kyauktada', in *Studies in British Imperial History*, ed. Gordon Martel, Macmillan 1986, p171.

15. Sigmund Freud, 'Psychoanalytic Notes on the Autobiographical Account of a Case of Paranoia' (1911[1910]), *Freud Pelican Library* 9, Penguin 1984, p204.

16. André Green, 'Projection', in *On Private Madness*, The Hogarth Press and The Institute of Psycho-Analysis 1986, p102.

17. Edward Said, *Orientalism*, Penguin 1991, p72.

18. Quote taken from an unpublished autobiography held in the School of Oriental and African Studies library archives.

19. David Bell, *Paranoia: Ideas in Psychoanalysis*, Icon Books 2002, p67.

20. David Goodhart, 'Discomfort of Strangers', *The Guardian*, 24.2.04.

21. Ibid.

22. See *Income and Wealth: Report of the JRF Inquiry Group*, The Joseph Rowntree Foundation 1995.

23. Goodhart, op cit.

24. Alasdair MacIntyre, *After Virtue*, Duckworth 1999, p222.

25. Hannah Arendt, *The Human Condition*, University of Chicago Press 1998, p59.

26. Paul Ricoeur, 'The Socius and the Neighbour', *History and Truth*, North Western University Press 1965, p98.

27. St Luke 10: 30-36, *The Bible*.

28. Giorgio Agamben, *Means Without End*, University of Minnesota Press 2000, pp22-23.

29. Jacques Derrida, 'On Cosmopolitanism', in *On Cosmopolitanism and Forgiveness*, trans. Mark Dooley and Michael Hughes, Routledge 2001, p7.

30. Paul Ricoeur, 'The Socius and the Neighbour', op cit, p99.

four | 'At war'

"Ungaretti
man of pain
all you do is an illusion
to give you courage"

Giuseppe Ungaretti

I've been reading novels and memoirs about war and I have been wondering why, and why now. In recent years a number of middle-aged men – the journalist Jeremy Paxman, the writers Robert Harris and Tony Parsons – have remarked how their generation, born in the 1940s and 1950s, have never been at war. Unlike their fathers, their courage and resilience was never put to the 'test'. The opportunity to prove themselves has passed them by. The idea that a man can discover his authentic self by going to war goes deep into the male psyche. It is not that men want war, but that for most of history men have lived under the expectation that it will be their fate. But there also exists in the nostalgia of these three men for the moral righteousness of the dutiful soldier a darker atavistic call from the European past: war makes man.

In my childhood, my father's old army dress uniform hung in the cupboard in my bedroom, and various items of military clothing were scattered through the house. An army great coat mouldered on a nail in the garden shed. On the window sill of the living room lay a silver cigarette case engraved with his name, a gift from his brother officers. He'd been a very young soldier called up for national service after the Second World War. He then stayed on and toured the colonial hot spots of the British Empire in its final days. I never found out what he did in these countries. My mother refused to be a soldier's wife and so he resigned his commission. The war, the army, were never spoken of, but during my boyhood they remained an ethereal, inescapable presence, and, for me, an endless source of fascination. Playing war was a favourite past time. Dressing up, stalking, shooting, carrying toy guns and throwing toy grenades, getting shot and coming back to life, collecting toy soldiers, reading comics and books and watching films about fictionalised wars, we manufactured a pretend world by drawing into ourselves the unspoken memories that pervaded the air we breathed. Somewhere in me there remains this fascination with the imaginary of war. In this essay I'm going to go in search of it and see where it takes me.

Episode 5 of the 2001 TV series *Band of Brothers* opens with the sound of a man's rapid, laboured breathing. He is running as fast as he is able and the camera jumps and bounds alongside him. There are flashes of his bayonet on his rifle, his boots, legs, body, the bayonet again, and then he is climbing up a short, steep bank. The camera lifts to a German soldier rising to his knees, a young boy who gives a momentary, diffident smile, as if the war does not exist and the sudden appearance of this stranger requires a polite welcome. The man fires his rifle and kills the boy. Paul Fussell has made a trenchant criticism of this kind of pseudo realism, which, he argues, romanticises and sanitises the unbearable folly and waste of the war: the GIs were all extremely young and very frightened, and their army profligate in getting them killed.[1] But for me this single scene of a singular murder momentarily tears the veil from the narrative of heroic sacrifice.

The Italian poet Giuseppe Ungaretti wrote of his generation's experience in World War One: 'Something in the world of languages is totally finished. We are men cut off from our own depths.'[2] And similarly, Walter Benjamin wrote of the same war: 'Was it not noticeable at the end of the war that men returned from the battlefield grown silent – not richer, but poorer in communicable experience.'[3] It is as if each new generation of young men must learn the ineffable nature of war. The same, predictable, thrill, terror and excitement corroding into the destruction of sensate experience. As Anthony Swofford describes it, the fighting comes to an end and those men still alive return home, but each remains at war with himself: 'the most complex and dangerous conflicts, the most harrowing operations, and the most deadly wars, occur in the head.'[4]

I will keep these insights in mind, because as I begin this essay I have a sense of entering our culture's disturbing, virtual world of warfare: a simulacrum of cinematic and televisual killing and destruction that is at once numbingly familiar and yet beyond our knowing. This paradox exploded into reality on 11 September 2001. I was part of a crowd that had gathered round a shop window to watch the World Trade Centre burning. When United Airlines Flight 175 crashed into the south tower I felt the symbolic order of the world I'd grown up in reverberate in shock. As the twin towers crashed to the ground something in my unconscious seemed to fall with them. In the days that followed I experienced a nostalgia for the TV-created America of my 1960s childhood. I recalled the programmes of small town, homespun innocence, fringed with the threat of disorder, that had formed my cultural imagination. In the loss I felt, I grasped for the first time the extent of my unconscious identification with America, formed in the English suburban middle class of my upbringing under the protective wing of its imperial power. The remnants of Empire my father had policed had given way to the Cold War and a brasher global hegemon. Its bloody borders, policed by executions and the torturing of enemies by proxies, its crushing economic exploitation and overthrowing of uncooperative governments, the sheer volume of the death and destruction that it employed – in order, it was claimed, to secure my way of life – had been transmogrified into all those sanitised Westerns in which the Indians bloodlessly bit the dust. War had become entertainment: a mediated, aesthetic experience that embellished death, and required a guilty innocence for its consumption.

In my hand is a games console. I press my finger on the forward button and the armoured car I occupy leaps forward toward an enemy checkpoint. I stop the vehicle and climb out. The digital landscape is North Korea sometime in the near future, inhuman in its functional anonymity. Streams of tracer erupt from the ant-like enemy soldiers. I lift my assault rifle and fire back. They fall like ants in their own small pools of blood. I climb back in and drive towards the clouds of smoke billowing on the horizon. This surreal world of computerised killing demands no courage or moral doubt, only sharp reflexes and quick thinking. As in modern warfare from 10,000 feet, death is an unimaginable distance away. Technological supremacy makes war remote. The West can avoid getting up close and personal to kill. Our legacies of imperial power ensure that our wars are fought 'over there', and men in post-industrial societies are disassociated from the death embracing culture of the warrior. But in the aftermath of 11 September we have entered a new era of global militarisation – the shadowed world of the War on Terror. It confronts us with the historical changes in men's relationship to war, and it opens up a new kind of front that needs investigating.

Goodbye to all that

In 1992, Norman Dennis and George Erdos wrote an apocryphal tract called *Families Without Fathers* for the Institute of Economic Affairs, a right-wing think tank. Men, they claimed, were evading their responsibilities as sexual partners and fathers. A generation of selfish and morally weak men, corrupted by permissive and liberal attitudes, had abandoned their wives and children. Numerous research projects and surveys of the last decade of the twentieth century catalogued a growing list of men's failings: the collapse of paternal authority, the rise of absent fathers, broken families and delinquent sons, the educational failure of boys, criminality, sexual immorality and promiscuity, suicide, and violence. In the media a consensus of opinion emerged about men as a gender. They were emotionally inarticulate, disoriented and demoralised. The post-industrial age of the information and service economy has undermined certain traditional ways of being male that were rooted in the industrial revolution and its domestic division of labour. Manuel Castells has described the emergence of trends which point towards the end of 'not just the nuclear family (a modern artefact), but the family based on patriarchal domination that has been the rule for a millennia'.[5] There are moments in history when an epochal social life draws to an end, and new values and forms of living begin to emerge.

Such metamorphoses do not burst upon people in sudden revelation. They are uneven, and affect some classes and groups more than others. They are hard to measure and quantify, but we nonetheless feel them profoundly. Such paradigmatic changes require a historical perspective.

Norbert Elias in *The Civilising Process* (1994) describes how technical and economic development has changed the position of the individual in society. Since the Middle Ages, interdependency between individuals has increased as the division of social functions has multiplied. The state has monopolised taxation and the use of violent force. Diverse regions, populations and centres of local power have been brought under a central form of stable government. The growing complexity of social functions and the process of integration have altered the way people are bonded together. This has produced changes in people's manners and in the structure of their personalities, most notably in the control of instinctual life: 'Through the interdependence of larger groups of people and the exclusion of physical violence from them, a social apparatus is established in which the constraints between people are lastingly transformed into self-constraints.'[6] Elias gives the example of the medieval knight whose personality was shaped by a life of perpetual danger, punctuated by brief moments of more protected existence. The knight lived in the immediate present with little mediation between his instinct and his social behaviour. His personality was characterised by sudden switches of mood. The pleasure of victory brought ecstatic joy. Danger, defeat or imprisonment was met with deep despondency (p448). Emotions were discharged openly and freely: 'but the individual was their prisoner; he was hurled back and forth by his own feelings as by forces of nature. He had less control of his passions; he was more controlled by them' (p452).

The transition from a feudal society marks the decline of this kind of impulsive, instinctual behaviour. 'Physical classes, wars and feuds diminish, and anything recalling them, even the cutting up of dead animals and the use of the knife at table, is banished from view or at least subjected to more and more precise social rules' (p453). People's bodily functions and sexual activities are hidden from view and bound by regulations and feelings of shame and embarrassment. As society becomes more pacific, individual sensitivity to social conduct becomes more acute: 'Continuous reflection, foresight and calculation, self-control, precise and articulate regulation of one's own effects, knowledge of the whole terrain, human and non-human, in which one acts, become more and more indispensable preconditions of social success' (p476). With the rise of a court society organised around the stable authority of a monarch, the sword gives way to intrigue and conflicts are contested with words (p475). As the state monopolises organised violence, the independent warrior caste of knights is made redundant.

The social development of self regulation and self constraint had the effect of moving the battlefield from the outside world to within. 'Inner fears grow in proportion to the decrease of outer ones – the fears of one sector of the personality for another' (p497). Tensions that were discharged directly in combat between man and man must now be resolved as inner tension in the struggle of the individual with himself. This increasing level of control over the body and instinctual life is evident in the asceticism of Puritanism and the rise of trade capitalism in the seventeenth century. Contracts required foresight, hindsight, calculation and trust. They established new forms of individualised relationships between men and replaced the rights, duties and reciprocities which had been a part of the patriarchal family. By the mid-nineteenth century, in England, the ideal of manliness, influenced by evangelical Christianity, was associated with public duty, honour, moral obligation and emotional restraint. These virtues were impersonal moral standards. How a man felt at any given moment was irrelevant to the question of how he should live. Manly codes of conduct – 'the stiff upper lip' – were intended to give order and meaning to men's lives. They expressed the values of the group and prescribed to the individual his role and what this required him to do. Middle-class manliness was a social role which provided society with its moral definitions.

Elias makes clear in his work that the civilising process has not been a one-way linear development, but has progressed in a long sequence of spurts and counter-spurts (p460). By the 1960s, Western societies were experiencing the peak of a deep-seated wave of informalisation. The virtues of duty and self-constraint were discredited as being too rigid and oppressive to assimilate the new individualised emotions, sexual identities and aspirations of an emerging consumer economy. Permissive legislation on divorce and sexuality undermined the styles of manliness and modes of power necessary to reproduce and sustain men's patriarchal, heterosexual role. By the late 1970s, and with the extraordinary leap in divorce rates, the institutional certainties of marriage could not longer be taken for granted. The language of love, trust and feelings was taking on a new importance in providing the framework within which people lived their lives. Women's struggle for independence meant that men had to negotiate their relationships with women and children on the basis of equality. The changes to men as a gender can be encapsulated in the paradigmatic shift from the historical ideal of manliness to the term masculinity which began to be used in the 1970s. Unlike the ideal of manliness, which was rooted in traditions of patriarchy, masculinity was conceived out of a breakdown in patriarchal relations. Men were no longer an unquestioned norm, they were being named as a gender.

Cas Wouters has explained this surge of democratisation, psychologisation and the informalising of conventional behaviour as a consequence of Europe's greater degree of physical safety and material security.[7] The beginning of this informalisation can be found in the publication of Freud's *The Interpretation of Dreams* in 1900, which marked a profound recognition of the previous centuries' civilising process of repressing instinctual behaviour. Wouters argues that since the late nineteenth century, successive generations, despite fascism and two global conflagrations, have been engaged in a long wave of informalisation, which has sought to diminish the intensities of shame, humiliation and loss of respect which have policed the repression of instinctual life inherited by the civilising process. This was a response to what Elias identified as the restlessness and dissatisfaction caused by the rigid demands of constraining, inhibiting and modifying instinctual life and emotions. 'The individual is no longer capable of any form of fearless expression of the modified affects, or of direct gratification of the repressed drives.'[8] Children grow up within social structures that anaesthetise particular instinctual drives or impulses. The fears and dangers which surround feelings associated with attachment, sexuality or childish hatred are so intense that they can remain unfelt for a lifetime.

The 1960s and 1970s marked the high point of the welfare state and a social democratic consensus that prioritised collective social security. With the growing influence of the neo-liberal economic order, the sharp rise in unemployment and an increasingly individualised society governed by market values, the informalisation and democratisation process was significantly slowed down. By the end of the 1980s, the fragmenting of public life and a prevalent social conformity had produced less social and more individual-centred personalities. Today we are living in a period in which competing ideas of what it means to be a man have reached a hiatus. The traditional personality structures, roles and values which had reached their apotheosis in the Victorian pater familias, and which had been subjected to repeated challenge in the 1960s and 1970s, re-emerge in new forms in various groups and individuals. Chauvinistic attitudes toward women surge back into social life. Struggles for equality go into abeyance. Such counter trends operate as a drag effect on the post-Victorian civilising process of informalisation and democratisation. Self-constraint and permissiveness, narcissism and social concern, tussle for primacy in the conflict between 'men's malleable drives and the built-in drive controls' (p487). Internal conflicts and contradictions find representation in culture. The repressed bursts into view. The May 1998 issue of the men's magazine *FHM* features a story 'Hell Hole', about Bang Kwang Prison in Thailand. A young Frenchman lies on his cell floor screaming in pain. There is a lump on his neck the size of an avocado, and the lump is moving. 'David lanced the lump with a razor blade. Out of the wound oozed hundreds of tiny wriggling worms, spilling out onto the cold stone floor like cooked spaghetti strands'. The July 1999 issue has a colour photograph of a 'devil's toe' – a congenital deformation of the foot. There is a picture of a 'half-man' born with only part of his spine and having had both legs amputated. A feature on 'Sport's Injuries' is illustrated with gored matadors, compound fractures and bloodied bodies. Deformation, bloodied insides, death, mutilation, corpses cut, carved, broken and burnt, the mess, dirt and stink of the human body are resurrected in every issue of *FHM* during this period.

Magazines, advertising, film and television, which had been sexualising images of the male body and divesting it of its trappings of formal authority, shift towards new representations of the male as self-possessed or dominant. The heroic body which had fallen into obloquy is resurrected. Films appear depicting extreme violence. In 1998, Marketing Consultants Mellors Reay and Partners produced a report *The State of Men,* which explained to advertisers how best to represent today's insecure man: 'In a world of confusion brands are a bedrock, a guarantee of continuity'. They suggest a 'local hero' campaign, which promotes the image of men in control. 'The outdoors nature of this approach is very macho – it's elemental, rugged, powerful. At best it's about escapism from this trapped life. It's about a taste of adventure, a feeling.' In conclusion they argue: 'The most successful way to communicate with men in today's environment is to reflect the soul of primal man. Man the warrior, the hero. In a world where men find their most basic instincts thwarted an advertiser who indulges their favourite fantasies should prosper.'

The quest for authentic male instincts is the theme of the film *Fight Club* (1999). 'We are a generation of men raised by women' says the main protagonist Tyler Durden, reflecting on marriage. 'I'm beginning to wonder if another woman is what we really need'. He founds a club where men can go and fight one another. The men in the Club strive to punch and batter each other into a recovered sense of masculine dignity. Be hit hard enough, hit back hard enough, and everything that a man has felt himself to be robbed of and shamed by will be put to rights. Morality is effeminate. Nothing counts except the male desire for authenticity. But what does it mean to be a man? Consumer culture has created a simulacrum of male experience. Men can dress in it, parody it, drink it, smoke it, watch it on TV, and drive the latest model of it. Tyler Durden makes money selling soap constituted from the fat lipo-suctioned from women's bodies. He wants to destroy commodity capitalism in order to feel himself alive. He does not want to destroy women. But in his rebellion to salvage his male pride, he is willing to reduce women's bodies to receptacles who produce fat he can exploit. His omnipotence is unsustainable, and he too is reduced to a commodity by his exploitative activities in an economic order that denies love, pleasure and intimacy in its pursuit of profit.

The celebration of the omnipotent male in popular culture is a symptom of the interregnum in the civilising process. It is a reaction against democratisation, and it resonates with archaic cultures of the warrior. The 1980s was characterised by the action films of Chuck Norris, Sylvester Stallone and Arnold Schwarzenegger, who each in their different ways sought vengeance on enemies who were sources of national or personal humiliation. Their hyper-masculinity was a protest against the informalisation process, which had denuded men of their power, status and authority. But they were idiosyncratic, adolescent heroes who pursued personal vendettas. They lacked the moral authority of manliness. A different kind of war story, reconnected to the nation and moral duty, made its appearance in the 1990s. The apparent reason was the anniversaries of the ending of the Second World War, and the various battles and events which shaped its course. Stephen Spielberg's film *Saving Private Ryan* (1998) was ostensibly made to commemorate the war generation of grandfathers, men close to the end of their lives. Its moral purpose, however, is to highlight the crisis of their sons and grandsons. Its realism is an attempt to represent an authentic experience of war fighting. But it is also a morality tale about our lost heroic virtues. Through the character of Corporal Timothy E. Upham it confronts post-war generations of men with a question about their own physical courage. How would you measure up? Upham is a young army clerk who finds himself enlisted as a translator to help Captain John Miller and his squad in their mission to find Private Ryan, a young soldier whose three brothers have all been killed in combat. Upham is an un-military, scholarly young man who holds a romantic view of war as an experience that bonds men together and provides a rite of passage into life's deeper meaning. But the violence he is exposed to proves to be an unbearable encounter with his own terror. Assigned to carry ammunition to a machine-gun post on the floor of a bombed out house, he is transfixed on the stairs by the sounds coming from the room above. Inside a German soldier and Upham's fellow GI are engaged in a desperate struggle to the death. The German is the stronger man. He overpowers his adversary and slowly plunges a knife into his heart. Emerging from the room, he walks down the stairs and contemptuously brushes past Upham, who, because he is incapacitated with fear, is unable to lift his rifle.

Saving Private Ryan depicts the primordial existence of a warrior society in which each man faces the imminent cessation of his being. What counts is his capacity to act in defence of his life. It is a recreation of the ancient, heroic world in which survival depended upon the individual knowing his role and knowing what this requires him to do. In this life and death struggle, a man's worth is measured by the honour conferred upon him by his peers. Each man is expected to know what he owes and what he is owed. The moral life of the individual is undifferentiated from the moral values of the group, his self no more than his role. Without this role he is neither recognised, nor will he know who he is. Any man attempting to disengage from his role will be conspiring in his own disappearance. To the German soldier descending the stairs Timothy Upham is without courage and so without honour. He is an invisible man who has no virtue. In contrast the virtuous man is Captain Miller, not simply because he possesses the necessary resilience, but because he moves steadily towards his own death. He is unafraid of his fate. As the film draws to an end, Miller is fatally wounded, and most of his soldiers are dead, sacrificed saving Private Ryan. Upham survives, and in one of the final scenes, under provocation, he shoots dead the German soldier who had passed him on the stairs.

In this brief scene, Spielberg reveals his own equivocal attitude toward an informalised, democratised society that he suspects has denuded men's heroic virtues. He perpetuates the myth of the warrior as everyman: war is a test. There is an echo here of the martial fantasies of the male will to power that generated the mentalities of European imperialism and fascism. At war, writes Ernst Junger, 'a man makes up for everything he has missed. At this point his drives, too long pent up by society and its laws, became once more the ultimate form of reality, holiness, and reason'.[9] Upham kills and so his manhood is confirmed and rescued from shame. Spielberg evades the horror of death prevalent in post-warrior Western societies. A similar effect is produced in Terrence Mallick's film *The Thin Red Line* (1998), in which war and killing are subsumed beneath a pseudo-mystical merging of man with nature. In their failure to confront the meaning of violent death, both films follow the trend of the earlier 'anti-war' movies like *Platoon* (1986), *Hamburger Hill* (1987) and *Full Metal Jacket* (1987), which represented a nation coming to terms with the Vietnam War. Death is displaced by action and the romanticism of heroic endurance. The iconic status of the Vietnam War was not simply based on its geopolitical significance in stalling US global hegemony and dividing a society. The war, as it was mediated by technology and as it was experienced by young conscripts, injected arbitrary and premature death and mutilation into the informalisation process of American consumer culture. As one daughter of a Vietnam veteran who committed suicide recalls: 'I can remember the entire family watching television each night to see which units were bombed and praying that it wasn't our dad's unit. What a cruel society we live in.'[10]

Where once death was feared but invested with a spiritual significance or a social function, informalisation has uprooted socially embodied structures of sacred meaning and left individuals alone to their fate. In post-industrial societies, where life has become less dangerous, the majority of individuals are no longer pushed to the margins of their existence by the continual proximity of death. It has been removed to the horizon of living, where it hovers just out of sight. As a consequence, it is lived as a state of perpetual anxiety without beginning or ending. The enemy is everywhere and nowhere. Viruses, disease, drugs, strangers and terrorists create a psychology of the terrorised. By the beginning of the twenty-first century, the processes of informalisation and democratisation in Britain and the United States had been stalled. Two decades of the neo-liberal economic order and its disciplinary forms of governmentality had created a sustained reaction against the emancipatory politics of the 1960s. US-led globalisation, driven by financial liberalisation, was faltering after the East Asia crisis and the onset of economic chaos in Argentina. A decade after the end of the

Cold War, the world was on the threshold of a new era of global militarisation.

The enemy will kill us

In 1999, George W. Bush warned America that it was living in 'an age of terror and missiles and madmen.'[11] Elected as President in 2000, he appointed Donald Rumsfeld as Secretary of Defence. Rumsfeld identified the dangers that lay ahead: 'the suitcase bomb, the cyber terrorist, the raw random violence of the outlaw regime'. The United States would stand against them. A new historic mission was dawning. What mattered more than material resources was 'character expressed in service to something larger than ourselves'.[12] In March, Paul Wolfowitz, the new Deputy Secretary of Defence, harkened back to the Second World War. In his Welcoming Ceremony speech he recited General Eisenhower's address to troops shortly before the D-Day Landings: 'You are about to embark on a great crusade. The eyes of the world are upon you.' Wolfowitz concluded his own speech: 'It is the same message that we might send to all those men and women in uniform doing America's work around the world today. "Free men of the world are marching together. I have full confidence in your courage and your devotion to duty. And let us all beseech the blessing of Almighty God upon this great and noble undertaking" '.[13] The rhetoric of the new Bush administration signalled a determination to assert control over the military and revive America's 'frontier spirit'. Manliness linked to a religious morality would rearm national pride and reverse the decadence of informalisation. The armed forces would spearhead a spiritual crusade for freedom.

William Kristol, one of the founders of the influential neo-conservative organisation, The Project for the New American Century, called for a 'foreign policy of American leadership and, yes, mastery'.[14] The Project's 2000 report *Rebuilding America's Defenses* – Wolfowitz had been a participant – detailed the war fighting capability and priorities needed to achieve that goal. But it wasn't until the terrorist attacks by Al Qaeda on 11 September 2001 that neo-conservative influence within the Bush administration established a new foreign policy. The crusading zeal intensified. 'This is not just America's fight', declared George Bush nine days after the attack, 'this is the world's fight ... This is civilization's fight.'[15] Rumsfeld told the official memorial service that the fight against terrorism would ensure that freedom became 'the birthright of every man, woman, and child on earth.'[16] A Global War on Terror was declared.[17] In January 2002, Bush identified an 'Axis of Evil' in his State of the Union address. The new Bush Doctrine contained three essential elements. 'Active American global leadership': the entire world is the battlefield and the enemy will be pursued wherever they are. 'Regime change': terrorist organisations and rogue regimes are targets in the war on terrorism. 'Promoting liberal democratic principles': no nation will be exempt from the 'non-negotiable demands' of liberty, law and justice.[18] America, Bush claimed, has been 'called to a unique role in human events.'[19] The Global War on Terror captured the providential spirit of the neo-conservatives.

A new enemy now assailed the Western imagination: Al Qaeda. Unknown and un-numbered, devoted to spiritual violence and in love with death. Bush described it as part of 'a terrorist underworld' that 'operates in remote jungles and deserts, and hides in the centers of large cities.'[20] Such a translucent enemy must be repeatedly named in order to give it substance. Richard Myers, the chairman of the Joint Chiefs of Staff described the threat – 'These folks are savages, mass murderers'.[21] Donald Rumsfeld was more expansive: 'It's not even really one particular organization. Rather it's a shifting network of fanatical adherents to violent extremism, and a movement that uses terrorism as its primary weapon of choice.' The enemy comes from a world that is pre-modern. 'They combine medieval views with modern tools and technologies. They operate within hostile and friendly nation-states and even within our own country.'[22] Philip Bobbitt likened Al Qaeda to the organisational structure of Visa or Mastercard – a mirror image of the institutions of global financial capital and the new Market State they have spawned.[23] But the more nuanced understandings of what Al Qaeda was, how it had emerged with US complicity, and the real nature of the military threat it posed, was drowned out by the vengeful lament that the barbarians had penetrated the walls of the city. 'A new age of barbarism is upon us', announced the 20 September 2004 editorial of *Business Week*. The terrorists have but one demand: 'the destruction of modern secular society'.

To mobilise popular support for the War on Terror a new official imaginary of war was created. Video games used for training US soldiers were tailored for the teen, civilian market. In 2002 *America's Army* was launched. Army spokesman Colonel Casey Wardynski, interviewed by the website www.gamespot.com, described the game's objective as putting the army into pop culture. It was an opportunity for teenagers to learn about the military. By May 2005 it had been downloaded over 5 million times. Alongside its release into civilian life, the game was being adapted as a training system for troops in Iraq. Known as the 'Common Remote Operator Weapons System', it was fielded in Iraq in the summer of 2005. Asked how it worked, Wardynski replied:

> Let's say these guys were somewhere in the Middle East, in Iraq, and they're at Camp Victory. They're going to train tonight and they're going to go out tomorrow and do real-world stuff. So tonight they hook up their tactical computer to the Hummer and pipe this stuff into their system and train. Tomorrow they unplug it, drive out and go do their business ... When they're training, they're using *America's Army*, and when they're doing it in the real world, they just turn *America's Army* off and use the equipment in a real-mode setting.[24]

America's Army creates the illusion of being an active participant in the War on Terror. From young teenage boys in suburban bedrooms to nineteen-year-old recruits in Baghdad, images and modes of perception are manufactured and shared in the construction of the enemy and his habitat. The civilian game is touched with the aura of a shared war experience. In the 2005 update, the bullets cause blood loss. Without a medic you will bleed to death over time. Life will ebb away – this is what it's really like. The simulacrum of fetishised technology and weaponry, and a frontier land of a collapsing Middle Eastern urbanscape, mythologises the pleasurable fantasies of being at war with the other: stalking, shooting, killing, but invulnerable in the face of death.

The official game website carries BLOGS from serving soldiers which fabricate a warrior mythology. Francis Marion is on his way to Firebase X:

> As I approach the firebase, I get the feeling of entering a medieval European castle with stone walls for its perimeter. Once inside it looks like they misplaced a Vietnam War movie set here with large green tents filling most of the spaces between the stone and concrete buildings ... Many of the Special Forces soldiers here are old friends and two of them were teammates on my last rotation to Afghanistan and I haven't seen any of them for about a year. The fellowship of soldiers who rely on each other for their daily safety is something few can understand, but Tolkien knew it and Shakespeare wrote about it when he penned 'we band of brothers'. It feels great to be back among them.[25]

Politicians delved into the same vocabularies to create an asinine boy's own adventure story. In a speech to a Heritage Foundation conference in 2004, Paul Wolfowitz depicted a war in Afghanistan that was a mixture of nineteenth-century, frontier Indian fighting, 1950s industrial modernity, and twenty-first century digital technology. Three paradigms of war appear in one battle for the strategic city of Mazar-e-Sharif.

> I had the honor and privilege of meeting with some of these young kids who had gone in in the very early days of the war ... At their first meeting with General Dostum, they weren't sure, they told me, whether he was going to kill them or embrace them. After the first embrace, fortunately, they were then told to get on horseback ... Only one of them had ever been on a horse in his life, and there they were off on a cavalry charge and within a very short time after that calling in B-52 strikes.[26]

Wolfowitz's story comes straight out of the Great Game of the British Empire, when the North West Frontier became the adventure playground for generations of English public school boys. The imagery is reproduced in the official narrative of US military action in Afghanistan:

> From the moment US Special Forces landed in Afghanistan, they began adapting to circumstances on the ground. They sported beards and

traditional scarves, and rode horses trained to run into machine gun fire, atop saddles fashioned from wood, with saddlebags crafted from Afghan carpets.

Together with the anti-Taliban forces they planned an assault on the strategically important city of Mazar-e-Sharif. After a hail of precision-guided bombs began to land on Taliban and al-Qaeda positions, hundreds of horsemen emerged, literally, out of the smoke, riding down on the enemy through clouds of dust and flying shrapnel. A few carried RPGs, some had less than ten rounds of ammunition in their guns, but they rode boldly, Americans and Afghans together, into tank, mortar, artillery and sniper fire. It was the first cavalry charge of the twenty-first century.[27]

In truth, Wolfowitz's 'young kids' were all men with an average age over 30. Stories emerged of pro-Taliban Pakistani fighters being shot dead after their surrender and of Northern Alliance gunmen 'roaming the streets' of the abandoned city. The journalist Robert Fisk dispels Wolfowitz's romantic yarn: 'The Uzbek, Tadjik and Hazara gunmen who make up this rag-tag army have a bloody reputation for torturing and executing prisoners which – if resumed in the coming days – will plunge America and Britain into a moral abyss.'[28]

The abyss

In his 1996 'Declaration of War against the Americans Occupying the Land of the Two Holy Places', Osama Bin Laden announced his fatwa with the opening words: 'Our youths believe in paradise after death. They believe that taking part in fighting will not bring their day nearer; and staying behind will not postpone their day either.'[29] Bin Laden confronted the West with its terror of death: 'Those youths are different from your soldiers. Your problem will be how to convince your troops to fight.' The vicarious thrills of computer war games and films like *Black Hawk Down* (2001) did not stir up a desire to fight in an actual war. In June 2005, and with the casualty rate in Iraq rising, the US army reported a growing recruitment and retention crisis.[30] The new imaginary of the War on Terror incited a paranoid dehumanising of the enemy. It projected out the repressed fears and instincts of the post-industrial societies and gave shape to a terrifying and dangerous world which harboured chaos, inhumanity and unrestrained hatred. In *Black Hawk Down*, Somali militiamen are portrayed as existing within the nihilistic embrace of death. One tells a captured American helicopter pilot: 'in Somalia killing is negotiation. There will always be killing ... This is the way things are in our world.' Mogadishu is depicted as a bankrupted Dantesque inferno, teeming with armed black multitudes driven by a singular desire, to kill Westerners. Here is the dark abyss beyond the borders of the American imperium. The lands without light, literally.

P.H. Liotta and James Miskel, two academics at the US Naval War College, use this metaphor of darkness to describe the new world order confronting the West.[31] In their work they reproduce NASA's image of the 'earth at night'. It is stark, intense and beautiful. Flows and grids of light punctuate the azure of the earth's surface, identifying the areas of economic development.[32] Liotta's and Miskel's interest in this photograph lies in the pockets of darkness: the Caribbean Rim, virtually all of Africa, the Balkans, the Caucasus, Central Asia, the Middle East and Southwest Asia, and much of Southeast Asia. These are lands which have been excluded from global flows of trade and capital, where soon half the population will be aged 15-29 and without employment or educational opportunities. Here, they write, are the 'feral zones' of under-governed remote rural areas, the semi-urbanised collections of displaced populations, the 'bubbling petri dishes' of the new arc of mega slum cities – Lagos-Cairo-Karachi-Jakarta – inside 'non-failing states', and the militia run 'para-states' which behave like zombies kept alive by injections of aid. In these places, they argue, lie the future threats to the United States. The solution is to intervene politically and economically and connect up these areas to the global economy. 'If September 11 taught us anything, it is that our security is inextricably connected to domestic governance shortcomings elsewhere.'[33]

The military-market complex

Charles Krauthammer had been less circumspect in his advocacy of intervention: 'America's involvement abroad is in many ways an essential pillar of the American economy'.[34] US global markets must expand to secure economic growth and ensure global security. This strategic role for markets in the War on Terror has been most forthrightly championed by Thomas P.M. Barnett, a former researcher with the Centre for Naval Analyses and, after 9/11, Assistant for Strategic Futures in the Office of Force Transformation. Like Liotta and Miskell, Barnett identifies the limits of globalisation as a key factor in US security:

> Show me where globalization is thick with network connectivity, financial transactions, liberal media flows, and collective security, and I will show you regions featuring stable governments, rising standards of living, and more deaths by suicide than murder ... These parts of the world I call the Functioning Core, or Core ... But show me where globalisation is thinning or just plain absent, and I will show you regions plagued by politically repressive regimes, widespread poverty and disease, routine mass murder, and – most important – the chronic conflicts that incubate the next genera-tion of global terrorists ... these parts of the world I call the Non-Integrating Gap, or Gap.[35]

The United States faces three tasks. First, it must 'bolster the Core's immune-system response' to 'disruptive perturbations' unleashed by events like 9/11. Second, it has to build a 'firewall' against Gap exports of 'terror, drugs, pandemics'. 'Seam states' – that lie along the Gap's 'bloody boundaries' – must be targeted: Mexico, Brazil, South Africa, Morocco, Algeria, Greece, Turkey, Pakistan, Thailand, Malaysia, the Philippines, and Indonesia. Third, it must steadily increase the export of security to the Gap's worst trouble spots. In conclusion, Barnett argues, the War on Terror will continue for decades. There are no exit strategies.[36]

In 2001, Barnett worked with the investment bank Cantor Fitzgerald to map out future relations between commerce and the military. His 'New Rules Set Project' involved national security policymakers, Wall Street financial institutions and academics. It identified a military-market complex that will facilitate a steady rise of connectivity between national economies and the outside world. Inward flows of private capital investment will utilise the 'inexpensive but dependable labour' of Gap countries. In turn such countries must develop 'good governance' and the enforcement of property rights and contracts. Barnett offers the example of Asia. In Asia, the commander-in-chief of US Pacific Command guarantees the security of the region: 'We trade little pieces of paper (our currency, in the form of a trade deficit) for Asia's amazing array of products and services. We are smart enough to know this is a patently unfair deal unless we offer something of great value along with those little pieces of paper. That product is a strong US Pacific Fleet, which squares the transaction nicely.'[37] But for Barnett it will be the private sector, not the state or the military, who will win the victories in the War on Terror – 'we don't need business to "get behind the war", but to get out in front of it'.[38]

Barnett's ideal of connectivity lacks historical perspective, and he ignores the dynamic of capitalism on which it depends. Capital accumulation and the pursuit of profit do not produce the collective, public goods necessary for sustainable and equitable development. Foreign Direct Investment (FDI) does not reduce inequality, nor does it deal with the causes of poverty. The military-market complex is a neo-liberal version of imperialism in which the spread of markets replaces the territorial ambitions of the nation state, and empire is partially denationalised. International finance capital, drawn from the metropolitan centres, moves to the periphery in search of lucrative returns. Rosa Luxemburg in 1913 described the role of the military in the historical process of capital accumulation. Militarism is used to 'forcibly introduce commodity trade in countries where the social structure had been unfavourable to it'; it turns 'the natives into a proletariat by compelling them to work for wages'; it creates and expands the spheres of interest for capital; and it 'enforces the claims of capital as international lender'.[39] Branko Milanovic of the World Bank has calculated that the richest 1 per cent of the world's population receive as much income as the bottom 57 per cent. The total income of the richest 25 million Americans is equal to the total income of almost 2 billion poor people.[40] History proves that market driven globalisation will not substantially alter the huge, global disparity in wealth. Milanovic argues that the first period of globalisation, from 1870 to 1913, occurred in a world of similar inequality. It culminated in the First World War, by which time the poor countries had fallen further behind, and the rich countries had become richer.[41]

C.P. Chandrasekhar and Jayati Ghosh, in their survey of the current global balance of payments, show how the private capital flows that Barnett envisages as creating connectivity and economic development, actually enforce the dependency of peripheral economies on the centre. They found that, 'private capital flowed into developing countries to earn lucrative returns, and this capital then flowed out as investment in low interest Treasury bills in order to finance the US balance of trade deficit'.[42] Financial liberalisation conscripts countries into a global financial system in service to the US economy. Korkut Boratav calculates that in 2003, the US economy benefited by up to $428 billions in net resource transfers from the rest of the world.[43] The military-market complex of the War on Terror penetrates non-marketised societies in order to secure extractive industries and sources of energy, and to construct a global market in labour and commodities. In the process it reverses the meagre political and economic gains made by countries in the process of decolonisation. The accompanying extreme violence – the 'collateral damage', the martial law, the renditions, state terror and destruction of infrastructure – expose a brutal set of rules generally overlooked by the pacific populations of the democratic metropolis. In 1853, Karl Marx described this colonial world when he wrote on British rule in India. 'The profound hypocrisy and inherent barbarism of bourgeois civilization lies unveiled before our eyes, turning from its home, where it assumes respectable forms, to the colonies, where it goes naked'.[44]

At war

Ernst Junger, made famous by his World War 1 memoir celebrating German militarism, was the archetypal warrior of destiny-driven, industrial modernity. He described himself as the son of an age intoxicated by materialism: 'progress seemed to us perfection, the machine the key to godliness, telescopes and microscopes organs of enlightenment. Yet underneath the ever more polished exterior, beneath all the clothes in which we bedecked ourselves, we remained naked and raw like men of the forest and the steppes.'[45] What was war to us, he asks. Giuseppe Ungaretti, caught in the same conflagration, had an answer, and in this answer lay the germ of the fascism he would later embrace. At war he believes that he springs from the same earth as the people: 'And in this your/soldier's uniform/I am at peace/as if it were my father's /cradle.'[46] Both men embrace war as the ultimate test of their manliness. War provides them with a sense of purpose and belonging.

For Robert Cooper, a more cautious British advocate of Barnett's neo-liberal imperialism, such martial fantasies – and Marx's barbarism – belong to the past. We live in a post-industrial economy dominated by services and an information sector. The state is no longer founded on the principle of violence: 'Hence its unwarlike character. War is essentially a collective activity. In the post modern state the individual is supreme.'[47] Individual consumption has replaced collective glory as the dominant theme of national life. 'War is to be avoided: empire is of no interest.'[48] But this is to fail to look beyond the domestic, to miss the violence involved in global capital accumulation.

Furthermore, as Elias has shown, the individual has a relationship to society that is a product of the interdependency of social functions and the integration under the state of dispersed sites of power. The notion of the supreme individual unconnected to social processes is not sustainable. The historic processes which shape our lives can be stalled or reversed, and the personality structure of the individual and the nature of the state can change. The neo-liberal economic order has fragmented communities, political associations and public identities. The social structures which once served to underpin democratisation have been weakened by market relations. What were once public goods are now measured by the criteria of cost and utility. And it is precisely this demise of the social, and the privatisation of the individual, that has provided the preconditions for the War on Terror.

Individuals of the post-industrial societies might be unwilling to sacrifice themselves for the destiny of the nation, but when their way of life appears threatened, there are other means of executing war which do not directly threaten them with death. The military-market complex, in Foucault's telling description of the bio-politics of the modern age, exercises the power to 'foster life or disallow it to the point of death'. Those populations living in Barnett's 'Gap' that are prepared to comply with its rule are included where needed in the global labour market; but those who will not play by the rules or who are simply superfluous, become, in Walter Benjamin's phrase, 'mere life'. Stripped of the identity and civic status of their social existence and without recourse to the law and the codes of civility of the state, such peoples are denied justice and mercy and can be killed with impunity. And when there is killing to be done, a denationalised imperialist war will find its proxies, mercenaries and private military firms to undertake the dirty work. The imperialism of the nation state will not return, but its neo-liberal marketised variant will draw for its sustenance upon its historic personality structures; it will update its militarism and liberalise its economics. We need to pay heed when we hear the atavistic call from our past.

NOTES

1. Paul Fussell, *The Boy's Crusade: The American Infantry in Northwestern Europe*, 1944-1945, Random House 2003.
2. Giuseppe Ungaretti in Andrew Frisardi, 'Giuseppe Ungaretti and the Image of Desolation', *Giuseppe Ungaretti Selected Poems*, Carcanet 2003, pxxvii.
3. Walter Benjamin, 'The Storyteller', *Illuminations*, Fontana 1992, p84.
4. Anthony Swofford, *Jarhead*, Scribner 2003, pp247-248.
5. Manuel Castells, *The Power of Identity*, Blackwell 1997, p139.
6. Norbert Elias, *The Civilising Process*, Basil Blackwell 1994 p332.
7. Cas Wouters, 'Formalization and Informalization: Changing Tension Balances in Civilizing Processes', *Theory Culture & Society*, Vol3, No2, 1986, pp1-18.
8. Elias, op cit, p454.
9. Ernst Junger, 'The War as Inner Experience' [1922], in *Fascism: A Reader*, trans. Roger Griffin, ed. Roger Griffin, Oxford University Press 1995, p109.

10. Suicide Wall, www.suicidewall.com/Suicide_Wall_results.asp?Key=6.

11. George W. Bush quoted in *Facing the Future: Meeting the Threats and Challenges of the 21st Century*, Office of the Assistant Secretary for Public Affairs, 2005, p29, www.defenselink.mil/pubs/facing_the_future/home1 .html.

12. www.defenselink.mil/speeches/2001/s20010126-secdef2.html.

13. www.defenselink.mil/speeches/2001/s20010316-depsecdef.html.

14. William Kristol, 'Foreign Policy and the Republican Future', *The Weekly Standard*, 7 September 1998, www.newamericancentury.org/defensenation alsecurity1998-1997.htm.

15. www.whitehouse.gov/news/releases/2001/09/20010920-8.html.

16. www.defenselink.mil/speeches/2001/s20011011-secdef.html.

17. Joint Senate Resolution 23. The Resolution limited the President's use of force to targets associated with Al Qaeda. The legal limitation did not dampen the global ambitions of the neo-conservatives. See www.law.cornell. edu/background/warpower/sj23.pdf: 'That the President is authorized to use all necessary and appropriate force against those nations, organizations, or persons he determines planned, authorized, committed, or   aided the terrorist attacks that occurred on September 11, 2001, or harbored such organizations or persons, in order to prevent any future acts of international terrorism against the United States by such nations, organizations or persons.'

18. Gary Schmitt, Tom Donnelly, 'Memorandum to Opinion Leaders "The Bush Doctrine"', www.newamericancentury.org/defense-20020130.htm, 30 January 2002.

19. www.whitehouse.gov/news/releases/2002/01/20020129-11.html.

20. www.whitehouse.gov/news/releases/2002/01/20020129-11.html.

21. www.defenselink.mil/news/May2005/20050530_1408.html.

22. www.defenselink.mil/news/May2005/20050525_1338.html.

23. Philip Bobbitt, excerpt from *War Against Terror*, Knopf 2005, www.utexas.edu/law/faculty/pbobbitt/waronterror/index.html.

24. www.gamespot.com/pc/action/americasarmystrykerovermatch/news_ 6124594.html.

25. *America's Army* official website, www.americasarmy.com/. See also www.riseofasoldier.com.

26. www.defenselink.mil/speeches/2004/sp20040227-depsecdef0241.html.

27. *Facing the Future: Meeting the Threats and Challenges of the 21st Century*, op cit, pp32-33; www.defenselink.mil/pubs/facing_the_future/home1.html.

28. Robert Fisk, 'What will the Northern Alliance do in our name now? I dread to think', *The Independent*, 14 November 2001.

29. Osama Bin Laden, 'Declaration of War against the Americans Occupying the Land of the Two Holy Places', www.mideastweb.org/osamabinladen1.htm.

30. Jamie Wilson, 'US army lowers standards in recruitment crisis', *The Guardian*, 4 June 2005.

31. P.H. Liotta, James F. Miskel, 'Redrawing the Map of the Future', *World Policy Journal*, March 2004, www.worldpolicy.org/journal/articles/wpj04-1/Liotta.pdf.

32. 'Earth at Night', http://apod.gsfc.nasa.gov/apod/ap020810.html.

33. P.H. Liotta, James F. Miskel, op cit, p20.

34. Charles Krauthammer, 'The Unipolar Moment', *Foreign Affairs 70*, 1991, p27.

35. Thomas P.M. Barnett, 'The Pentagon's New Map', *Esquire*, March 2003.

36. Thomas P.M. Barnett, *The Pentagon's New Map*, G.P.Putnam 2004, p179.

37. Thomas P.M. Barnett, 'Asia: The Military-Market Link', *The U.S. Naval Institute*, January 2002, pp53-56, www.thomaspmbarnett.com/published/atmml.htm.

38. Thomas P.M. Barnett, 'The Top Ten Reasons Why I Hate World War 1', *Newsletter from Thomas P.M. Barnett*, April 25 2005, p9, www.thomas pmbarnett.com/weblog.

39. Rosa Luxemburg, 'Chapter 32 Militarism as a Province of Accumulation', *The Accumulation of Capital*, 1913, www.marxists.org/archive/luxemburg/1913/accumulation-capital/ch32.htm.

40. Branco Milanovic, 'True World Income Distribution, 1988 and 1993: First Calculation Based on Household Surveys Alone', *The Economic Journal*, 112 (January), 2002, pp88-89, www.yale.edu/unsy/Occasional_Lectures_Milanovic.pdf.

41. 'Inequality in the World Economy by the Numbers: An interview with Branko Milanovic', *Multinational Monitor*, Vol 24, No7&8, 2003, http://multinationalmonitor.org/mm2003/03july-aug/july-aug03toc.html.

42. C.P. Chandrasekhar and Jayati Ghosh, 'The New Structure of Global Balances', November 2004, http://networkideas.org/news/nov2004/news11_Global_Balances.htm

43. Korkut Boratav, 'Some Recent Changes on the Relations Between the Metropoles and the Periphery of the Imperialist System', paper presented at the Conference on The Economics of the New Imperialism, New Delhi, January 2004, p5, www.networkideas.org/feathm/feb2004/ft03_IDEAs_Delhi_Conference.htm.

44. Karl Marx, 'The Future Results of British Rule in India', *New-York Daily Tribune*, 8 August 1853, www.marxists.org/archive/marx/works/1853/07/22.htm.

45. Ernst Junger, op cit.

46. Giuseppe Ungaretti, 'Italy', *Selected Poems*, op cit, p51.

47. Robert Cooper, *The post-modern state and the world order*, Demos 2000 p31, www.demos.co.uk/catalogue/thepostmodernstate/; See also Robert Cooper 'Why we still need empires', *Observer*, 7 April 2002, http://observer.guardian.co.uk/worldview/story/0,11581,680117,00.html.

48. Ibid, p32.

49. Michel Foucault, *The History of Sexuality An Introduction*, Penguin, 1986, p138.

50. Walter Benjamin, 'Critique of Violence', *One Way Street and Other Writings*, Verso, 1985.

five | Earthbound

On my shelf is a small piece of obsidian. It is igneous rock – like olivine, rhyolite and basalt – and it evolved out of the formation of the earth which began some 4.6 billion years ago. Molten lava exploded onto the earth's surface and came into contact with water. Its rapid cooling means that it has no crystalline structure. Obsidian's polished surface is like dark glass. Fracture it and let your thumb lightly slide across the sharp edges. Prehistoric societies used it to make cutting instruments, weapons and jewellery. It is an example of nature becoming culture, a reminder that the two are indivisibly bound together. Multicellular animals originated in the Cambrian period 530 million years ago. Upright primates emerged between two and four million years ago on the African Savannah to evolve into our ancestors. Human beings are the consequence of chance, contingency, thousands of unpredictable states. There is no timeless law of nature that has brought us here to this point in time. Humanity on earth is a firefly in dimensions of time and space incomprehensible in their size. Our fate is inextricably bound to that of our planet, and yet we have come to repudiate this fact. A mere two hundred years of industrial production and consumption by a fraction of the human population has despoiled the earth and brought us to the limit of its carrying capacity. Like a destructive oedipal drama, modernity has dedicated itself to escaping the confinement of the earth. Its triumphal march forward and constant revolutionising of the instruments and relations of production have refuted all limits. With the European enlightenment, the appeal to god the father to lift us skyward and grant us immortality was replaced by a faith in scientific progress that would liberate us from our earthly mortal lives. The present became infused with the idea of unlimited enrichment and advancement. The future would take care of itself, death is banished to the far horizon of life.

This morning I walked down my street which is overcrowded with cars. The sun was struggling to emerge from the clouds, people were leaving their houses for work, a few children were early for school. Nothing here in this urban environment – the tarmac road and concrete pavement, the houses built circa 1860, the noise of the traffic squeezed into the nearby main road – seems to connect to the geological time and nature of the earth. The shops are stocked with factory produced foodstuffs. Plastic wrapped pieces of meat and uniform-looking vegetables devoid of blood and dirt are denuded of their origins. It is as if this life has only a tenuous connection to the natural world and is answerable to none of its laws. The goal of modernity has been the destruction of our earthliness and the creation of a world of human artifice. A charade that denies our interdependency, as if without the oil, natural gas, fresh water, soil, precipitation, ocean currents, oxygen of the biosphere, our human artefacts could continue to be produced, traded and consumed. Like many others in this street, the house I live in moves as the clay it is built on shrinks in the drier weather. As the house moves its walls crack; vertical lines from floor to ceiling, diagonal lines, horizontal, criss-crossing patterns. The cracks are intimations of structural damage. They require measuring and monitoring. The future develops an element of uncertainty. The exceptional heat of recent summers, the freakish storms, the floods, the aberrant pattern of the seasons, the reports of distant weather-related disasters, take on a darker hue. Are they harbingers of a profound loss? Not just of the greenery of trees, the pleasures of the seasons, the unremarkable presence of fresh water, but life itself?

In 1958, at the beginning of the space age, Hannah Arendt published her book *The Human Condition*. She began by noting the sentiment carved on the funeral obelisk of the early Russian space pioneer Tsiolkovsky: 'Mankind will not remain bound to the earth forever'. This cosmic destiny was apocryphal: 'Should the emancipation and secularisation of the modern age, which began with a turning away, not necessarily from God, but from a god who was the Father of men in heaven, end with an even more fateful repudiation of an Earth who was the Mother of all living creatures under the sky?' Her book had a simple task: 'it is nothing more than to think what we are doing.'[1] A little over ten years later, on 16 September 1969, astronaut 'Buzz' Aldrin, the man who followed Neil Armstrong to walk on the moon, addressed a joint session of the US Congress.[2] During the flight of Apollo 11 the spacecraft had to be kept cool by slowly rotating it. 'As we turned, the earth and the moon alternately appeared in our windows. We had our choice. We could look toward the Moon, toward Mars, toward our future in space – toward the new Indies – or we could look back toward the Earth, our home, with its problems spawned over a millennium of human occupancy.' Aldrin eulogises the frontier spirit of America – 'Man has always gone where he has been able to go. It is that simple'. But, he says, there is also mystery and uncertainty. The earth is heading towards an unknown destination in the cosmos, travelling many thousands of miles per hour in the direction of the constellation Hercules: 'Where are we going?'.

What are we doing and where are we going?

In October 2003, an unclassified report, *An Abrupt Climate Change Scenario and Its Implications for United States Security*, was published by the Pentagon. It had been written by Peter Schwartz, a CIA consultant and former head of planning at the Royal Dutch Shell group, and Doug Randall of the Global Business Network.[3] Andrew Marshall of the Office of Net Assessment, the Pentagon's secretive think tank, had commissioned it. Its task was to imagine the unthinkable. It wasn't until February 2004 that *Fortune* magazine ran a scare story.[4] *The Observer* followed with its own version two weeks later.[5] Despite the initial lack of media interest, Marshall's legendary status as the octogenarian architect of US post-war military strategy gave the report status and significance.

The two authors had studied the various models of predicted climate change, gathered the scientific evidence, compared arguments, assessed dissension within the scientific community, and then amalgamated it all into their own 'climate change scenario for the future'. They stated that, 'there appears to be general agreement in the scientific community that an extreme case like the one depicted below is not implausible' (p7). Theirs is a dystopian vision. By 2020 Europe will witness an increasing number of armed skirmishes over water and immigration. France and Germany will clash over access to the Rhine. Severe drought and cold will have created a southward migration from Scandinavian countries. People begin to leave from Holland and Germany and increasing numbers of Europeans migrate to North Africa, Israel, Egypt. In Asia, the situation is much more dangerous. There is persistent conflict between Burma, Laos, Vietnam, India and China. In China civil war breaks out. Tension grows between China and Japan over access to Russian energy sources. The United States has retreated into isolationism, but its oil supply is threatened by conflicts in the Persian Gulf and Caspian. Disagreements over water with Canada and Mexico have created serious tensions, and its borders are assailed by huge numbers of refugees escaping the deteriorating situation in Mexico and the Caribbean islands. 'As famine, disease, and weather-related disasters strike due to abrupt climate change, many countries' needs will exceed their carrying capacity. This will create a sense of desperation, which is likely to lead to offensive aggression in order to reclaim balance' (p18). The authors conclude their report: 'Disruption and conflict will be endemic features of life' (p22).

Schwartz and Randall are making a prediction.[6] Climate change is about the future. Or rather it is about a future that no longer fits the story of modernity. It has become vulnerable to our present day activities. It can no longer take care of itself. Faced with the prospect of serious and dangerous changes in the global patterns of weather, scientists have built models of the future based on the calculation of complex sets of data. These relate to demographic and environmental trends, developments in technology, contrasting scenarios of economic growth, energy use and consumption, and differing political responses to the impact of climate change. In 2000, the Intergovernmental Panel on Climate Change (IPCC) published a 'Special Report on Emissions Scenarios'.[7] It sets out six illustrative emissions scenarios which provide alternative trajectories for greenhouse-related gases for the period 1990 to 2100. Their storylines form the parameters of a broad consensus of agreement amongst world scientists. The IPCC's Third Assessment Report (2001) confirms that human activities have increased the atmospheric concentrations of greenhouse gases and aerosols since the pre-industrial era.[8] The atmospheric concentration of CO_2 for the period 1000-1750 was 280 parts per million (ppm). In 2000 it was 368ppm. Meanwhile the global mean surface temperature had increased by 0.6°C (plus or minus 0.2°C) during the twentieth century, greater than that for any other century in the last thousand years.[9]

The subsequent regional changes in climate have had significant effects. Non-polar glaciers are in widespread retreat. Permafrost has thawed or is warming and degraded. The duration of ice cover on lakes and rivers in the mid- and high-latitudes of the northern hemisphere has lessened by about two weeks. Snow cover has decreased. The global mean sea level has increased at an annual rate of 1 to 2mm during the twentieth century. Mid- to high-latitude growing seasons have lengthened. Severe storms have increased in number with an associated rise in weather-related economic losses. There has been a poleward and altitudinal shift of plant and animal ranges, the decline of some plant and animal populations, and earlier flowering of trees, emergence of insects, and egg-laying in birds.[10] By 2100, the six illustrative SRES scenarios project concentrations of CO_2 in the range of 540-970 ppm. These will trigger potentially dangerous changes in the physical and biological systems of the earth. Some will be irreversible. Global temperatures are likely to rise by between 1.4 and 5.8°C during the twenty-first century.[11] Extreme weather conditions will become more frequent – the summer of 2003 was probably the hottest in Europe since the sixteenth century and was the cause of a significant number of heat-related deaths.[12] The International Energy Agency's 2004 World Energy Outlook sounded a warning. 'If governments stick with the policies in force as of mid-2004, the world's energy needs will be almost 60 per cent higher in 2030 than they are now.[13] CO_2 emissions will be more than 60 per cent higher.

In February 2005, the UK government sponsored an 'International Symposium on the Stabilisation of Greenhouse Gas Concentrations'. Its report revealed that, 'in many cases the risks are more serious than previously thought'.[14] In the absence of government action the global temperature will rise by between 0.5°C and 2°C by 2050. To prevent this happening and limit the global mean temperature to 2°C above present-day levels will require limiting the concentration levels of CO_2 to between 490ppm and 670ppm. This will mitigate some but not all dangerous climate changes. C.G. Rapley of the British Antarctic Survey reports that, 'recent climate change shows a very rapid warming of the climate in the Antarctic Peninsula region over the last 5 years'.[15] Seventy-five per cent of its 400-plus glaciers are in retreat. If global temperatures rise above 3°C, the ice sheets of the Antarctic will be destabilised. The Arctic is much more vulnerable. In 2005, the earth observatory at NASA reported a record low for June Arctic ice.[16] According to the research of the UK's Hadley Centre, a rise of 1.5°C will cause the Greenland ice sheet, which contains around three million cubic kilometres of ice, to begin to melt. A complete meltdown taking millennia would then be inevitable.[17] The Centre predicts that even with the lowest carbon emissions scenario, about 60 per cent of Arctic sea ice will be lost by the end of the century. If the climate can be stabilised, there will be a continuing loss of summer sea ice, with about 25 per cent still remaining in 2200. The subsequent rise in sea levels will threaten whole populations living in low-lying areas. And as the ice melts to create larger expanses of surface seawater global warming will intensify. Sea ice helps cool the earth by reflecting solar radiation back into space. Seawater with its darker surface absorbs the heat. In the longer term the complete melting of the Greenland ice sheet will raise sea levels by seven metres.[18]

In May 2005, *The Times* reported that Britain faced the prospect of severe, Siberian winters.[19] A principal cause of this regional climate change was the melting Arctic ice. Peter Wadhams, professor of ocean physics at Cambridge University, claimed that increasing levels of fresh melt water were affecting the North Atlantic thermohaline circulation which brings warmer temperatures to Britain. The thermohaline circulation is a mechanism by which the oceans import and export vast quantities of heat and salt.[20] In the Gulf of Mexico, warm upper layers of the ocean are driven northward by winds, creating the Gulf Stream which turns into a flow of water known as the North Atlantic Drift. At the same time, several kilometres below the surface, a mass of cold salty water known as the North Atlantic Deep Water flows southward. In the Labrador Sea and between Greenland, Iceland and Norway, these two layers are overturned in a pump-like operation. The warm surface water is cooled by cold winds and becomes more saline. As it becomes denser it sinks, displacing the existing deep flow of cold water and pushing it southward. Wadhams claims that increasing quantities of freshwater ice melt is decreasing the density of the flows and slowing down the thermohaline circulation. Evidence from Bill Turrell of the Ocean Climate Group has proved a decrease in the salinity of water flowing south, and Bogi Hansen of the Faroes Fisheries Laboratory has confirmed this trend. The level at which the water is 0.5°C sank by 60 metres between 1988 and 1997, a significant drop in the quantity of dense cold water.[21]

If the thermohaline circulation comes to a halt, central England will regularly experience daily winter temperatures below -10°C. The circulation collapsed once before, during the Young Dyas period 13,000 years ago, when the temperature over Greenland fell below -50°F, beginning a cold period that persisted for over 1000 years. The Hadley Centre dismisses this scenario and projects that by the middle of the century the Gulf Stream will have slowed down by about 20 per cent.[22] However, research by other scientists concludes that in the absence of a global climate policy the likelihood of a collapse of the Atlantic thermohaline circulation between now and 2205 is 50 per cent. With policy intervention there is a greater than 25 per cent likelihood of collapse.[23]

Much of the uncertainty about the future impact of climate change involves the capacity of existing natural processes to remove CO^2 from the atmosphere. A large amount of carbon dioxide emitted by fossil fuel burning is absorbed by natural 'sinks', which include phytoplankton in the oceans, forests, vegetation, soil, and tundra. Carbon can be stored in roots, wood, leaves. These natural sinks have helped to slow down climate change. However global warming and environmental degradation are reducing their capacity to absorb carbon. Increasing numbers of forest fires, massive deregulated and illegal logging, and land use changes for cattle production and urban development, are destroying carbon sinks and releasing their stored carbon into the atmosphere. And as temperatures rise and rainfall decreases, vegetation is dying back. The oceans too are affected. Their rising levels of CO^2 concentrations increase their acidity and diminish their capacity for absorption. The Hadley Centre calculates that the vegetation sink will start to collapse later in this century and will become a net source of carbon. By the end of the century 75 per cent of the carbon stored in the Amazon rain forest will have gone, released into the atmosphere.[24] This may prove to be an optimistic view. Research at the UK's National Soil Resources Institute suggests that higher temperatures have intensified the rates of decomposition of organic material in British soils.[25] This increases the carbon released into the atmosphere to well beyond current estimations. The Institute calculates that since 1978, 13 million tonnes of carbon per year have been dispersed into the atmosphere. The amount exceeds the 12.7 million tonnes annual reductions in emissions achieved between 1990 and 2002 that was part of Britain's commitment to the Kyoto Protocol. (In a separate study, this official estimation of reduction is disputed by Friends of the Earth.[26]) Guy Kirk of the Institute says: 'The buffering effect of soils mopping up emissions is not as strong as we expected. The scary thing is that the amount of time that we have to do something about climate change is now smaller.' His warning pales beside George Monbiot's estimation in his 2006 book *Heat* that global temperatures will rise by 2°C by 2050 unless the rich countries of the world reduce their carbon emissions by 90 per cent.

Industrial capitalism has built a life founded on the manufacture of waste. What is superfluous to the operation of the market becomes invisible.

It is consigned to the past without present or future. We have created societies beyond nature. Once tamed and despoiled, nature makes its reappearance as a cultural object of veneration, its landscapes an ideological confirmation of timeless national traditions and the status quo. What wilderness survives becomes a source of authenticity and rugged individualism. In the instrumentalist tradition of modernity, the natural world has been seen as an object to be appropriated, its resources there for the taking. In the capitalist market it is an externality, and thus discounted from the calculation of profit and loss: a huge dustbin for the detritus of production and consumption. For the Romantics of the eighteenth century, in rebellion against the emerging industrial revolution, nature was the counter to the dehumanising machine age. It was the source of life: 'A motion and a spirit, that impels/All thinking things, all objects of all thought,/And rolls through all things'.[27] From this dissenting tradition emerged counter movements against modernity and modernisation – mainstream environmental organisations for whom 'the environment' is an object of policy, and counter cultural movements seeking a more 'natural life'. Both the mainstream and the more radical parts of the movement appeal to justice to end the exploitation of nature. But the sociologist Klaus Eder argues that this appeal fails: 'Injustice to nature is an insufficient motivation for people to question the basic premises of their relation to it.'[28] The problem is our symbolic relationship to nature and it goes beyond the scope of justice.

This dilemma is not confined to our relationship to nature. It belongs also to our relationship to human biological life. Like non-human living organisms, humanity too can become waste. Industrial capitalism, in creating a commodity labour market in the nineteenth century, structured surplus labour as an externality that was excluded from the costings of business. The Poor Law Reforms of 1834 ruthlessly enforced the commodification of labour by removing the poor's 'right to live'. The historical challenge to this system came from the counter movements of socialism and communism. They ameliorated its worst effects, but on achieving power in the twentieth century they also reproduced the instrumentalist logic of modernity, reducing nature to an object to be incorporated into production. The logic of capital accumulation is to appropriate non-commodity social forms and relations in order to turn them into marketable goods. Once their value is extracted they are turned into waste products. As liberal market capitalism becomes a globalising dynamic destroying traditional economies, large swathes of humanity are rendered superfluous to requirements. Countless human beings become suspended in a state of social death. Deprived of their citizenship and identity it is as if they are reduced to a state of nature. Life without legal or political representation has a precarious existence in human society.

The separation of nature from society and the biological body from social identity has driven a modern dynamic of destruction. Humanity is close to the limit of the earth's capacity to carry us and absorb our activities. It may already have surpassed that moment. The relationship between natural life and society needs to be re-imagined. We need to found society in nature and establish a new kind of relationship between biological life and the social discourses, civic cultures, economic priorities, and jurisprudence of modernity.

Naked life

The Ancient Greeks made a distinction between biological life and cultural and political life, and this distinction has shaped our historical understanding of what constitutes morality and politics. The term *zoe* expressed the simple living body, and the term *bios* signified forms of life that were independent of necessity and so constituted freedom. Aristotle identified three prominent forms of life: the life of enjoyment and pleasure, the political life, and the contemplative life.[29] These forms of life could only be pursued in full independence from the labour required to keep one's self alive. The labour to satisfy the needs of the body and the reproduction of life was the work of women and slaves and was incompatible with citizenship and participation in public affairs. Freedom, legality, the political, the sphere of free and moral men, all this was dependent upon the household but only commenced outside its walls. Within the household, force and violence were justified as the means to master necessity. From the beginning, the idea of freedom and independence from necessity were inseparable from violence.

The distinction between *zoe* and *bios* has remained central to the operation of political power in modern western societies. At the heart of our political traditions is an ambivalence about the value of life and the respect accorded it by political sovereignty. The American Declaration of Independence of 1776, which declared that all men are created equal and endowed with the inalienable rights of life and liberty, nonetheless inaugurated a slave state. The French Revolution's 1789 Declaration of the Rights of Man reproduced the separation of *zoe* and *bios* by promoting the universal rights of Man but limiting the guarantee to a national citizen's law. Walter Benjamin addresses the distinction between lived life and law in his essay 'A Critique of Violence'. Violence, he argues, is an integral element of juridical law-making. In the moment a law is instated violence is not deposed; a law does not become an end immune and independent from violence but one which is intimately and necessarily bound up with it. In his attempt to understand the nature of juridical power over individual life Benjamin has to try and conceptualise this relationship. To do so he introduces the term 'mere' or 'naked' life, which describes the bearer of the link between violence and the law. Naked life depicts the human being stripped of identity and civic status. 'With mere life', Benjamin writes, 'the rule of law over the living ceases.'[30]

The right of human beings to life survives only so long as there exists a political community willing and able to guarantee it. To be stateless is to risk being expelled from humanity. In the wake of Benjamin, the philosopher Giorgio Agamben has attempted to overcome the historical distinction between *zoe* and *bios* by giving naked life a new kind of political potentiality. His essay 'Form-of-Life' (2000) is an attempt to think what the *bios* of *zoe* might mean. He argues that the historical separation of *zoe* and *bios* needs to be brought to an end in a single indivisible term – 'a life that cannot be separated from its form, a life in which it is never possible to isolate something such as naked life'.[31] What is at stake in such a life is not its particular form, but living itself. Naked life has been the hidden foundation of political sovereignty, but now, Agamben argues, naked life has become the dominant form of life everywhere (p6). The division between 'man' and 'citizen' established with the Declaration of the Rights of Man has been superseded by the division between naked life and identity. Following Foucault, he argues that a new kind of bio-political exercise of power has emerged in the medical-scientific ideologies that administrate the life of populations. An increasing medicalisation of our lives results in naked life giving way to biological life. Forms of life become forms of survival. In the light of these developments, he asks, 'Is today something like a form-of-life, a life for which living itself would be at stake in its own living, possible?' (p9).

Agamben's question owes much to Heidegger's philosophy and his attempt to understand the nature of 'Being'. Heidegger challenges the idea, central to Western science and metaphysics, that understanding something can be achieved by reducing it into separate elements for analysis. The world is more than the sum of its parts. Western modernity has created instru-mental, technical and objectifying mode of thinking, in which thought attempts to assert mastery and control over the world. Heidegger's interest is in the whole that precedes the parts, and in our pre-theoretical, non-reflective, intuitive attunement to this world: what he describes as our 'being there' (Dasein). The natural world does not exist separate from humanity. Self and world, inner and outer, are not counterposed to one another. Together they constitute the structure of 'being-in-the-world'. For Heidegger, 'world' does not refer to an actual object like the planet. It is the intuitive sense of the space of our living, which is created out of our percep-tions and conceptions of the objects and beings which make themselves known to us.

> World is the ever-nonobjective to which we are subject as long as the paths of birth and death, blessing and curse, keep us transported into Being. Wherever those decisions of our history that relate to our very being are made, are taken up and abandoned by us, go unrecognised and are rediscov-ered by new inquiry, there the world worlds. [32]

Heidegger seeks to give this intangible 'worlding' a material sense of its time and place. To do this he introduces the word 'earth': 'Earth is that which comes forth and shelters. Earth, self-dependent, is effortless and untiring. Upon the earth and in it, historical man grounds his dwelling in the world' (p46).

The dualism of earth and world appears to be similar to the ancient distinction between *zoe* and *bios*, in which earth is a limitation, the representation of necessity. But Heidegger is questioning the fundamental assumptions of our knowing and understanding, and he avoids this distinction. World and earth are not separate, opposing entities.

> World and earth are essentially different from one another and yet are never separated. The world grounds itself on the earth, and the earth juts through the world. But the relation between world and earth does not wither away into the empty unity of opposites unconcerned with one another. The world, in resting upon the earth, strives to surmount it. As self-opening it cannot endure anything closed. The earth, however, as sheltering and concealing, tends always to draw the world into itself and keep it there (p49).

The relationship takes the form of a striving, in which each opponent raises the other into the self-assertion of their natures (p49).

> The earth cannot dispense with the Open of the world if itself is to appear as earth in the liberated surge of its self-seclusion. The world, again, cannot soar out of the earth's sight if, as the governing breadth and path of all essential destiny, it is to ground itself on a resolute foundation (p49).

To read Heidegger is to enter a poetics which attempts to rethink the 'destitute time' of European modernity and find another kind of symbolic relationship between human beings, and between human beings and the natural world. His challenge is revolutionary, but one which is filled with ambiguity.

Heidegger's deconstruction of the West's 'technical interpretation of thinking' can lead to a disturbingly reactionary language, one which idealises the mythical peasant life of the soil. In his search for a sense of belonging in an authentic, historical community, Heidegger willingly surrenders the individual to a greater power. To read Heidegger is to glimpse a world in which human beings might discover a new kind of dialogue with each other. And at the same time it is to be reminded of why Heidegger flirted with the racial, volk fantasies of Nazism. It is as if Heidegger's philosophy can tip either way; into freedom or into a form of enslavement. His work manifests the conflict between 'the human' and the political community, and between life and the economic; these, with all their ambiguities, lie at the heart of the fraught, often deadly political heritage of modernity. They can be understood as the modern condition of the ancient historical struggle between *zoe* and *bios*, necessity and freedom. Overcoming this distinction remains central to rethinking politics and the nature of human being. Such a task requires paradigmatic changes in the conceptual frameworks we use to apprehend the world.

The shape of life

Historically, new conceptual frameworks have been precipitated by new scientific knowledge, which throws into disarray existing understandings of the world. In 1943, the physicist Erwin Schrodinger gave a series of lectures at Trinity College, Dublin, which were published as a small book, *What is Life?*. The question he addressed was: 'How can the events in space and time which take place within … the spatial boundary of a living organism be accounted for by physics and chemistry?'[33] Schrodinger begins with the second law of thermodynamics. The first law of thermodynamics states simply that energy within a system is conserved. The second law is about the instability of living systems, which are characterised by the flux of energy and matter passing through them. Living systems lack equilibrium. Energy that is localised in matter spontaneously disperses. Matter goes from a state of order to disorder – hot objects cool down, human beings lose heat generated by their metabolic activity. It is possible to store and conserve energy, but it is not possible to recover it once it has been used. The second law states that there is a direction to this dispersal of energy. It is running down. This movement is known as entropy. Entropy is the measure of disorder created by the dispersal of energy. Where there is life there is greater order and so lower entropy. As an entity decays and gives out more energy than it takes in, entropy increases.

Schrodinger describes the characteristic of matter which is alive as its capacity to exchange material with its environment. 'When a system that is not alive is isolated or placed in a uniform environment, all motion usually comes to a standstill very soon. The whole system fades away into a dead, inert lump of matter. A permanent state is reached, in which no observable events occur.'[34] This equilibrium is 'maximum entropy'. Living organisms produce entropy through bodily exertion and metabolic activity and so they are constantly moving towards a state of equilibrium and death. They stall this process because they are able to regulate their internal entropy by drawing in negative entropy from the surrounding environment. In other words food, which is ordered matter. By taking in orderliness from its environment, a living organism maintains itself in a stationary state at a fairly high level of orderliness (a low level of entropy). It escapes decay into atomic chaos by concentrating a 'stream of order' onto itself through a small number of highly ordered chromosome molecules. Living systems are order created out of ordered matter in a universe heading toward equilibrium. Life is the exception to the rule of the second law of thermodynamics.

Living and non-living systems share in common what the chemist Ilya Prigogine calls 'dissipative structures'. 'Dissipative structures' are self-created out of surpluses of energy, and maintain the order of a system. They have structure but no permanence and they dissipate when the supply of energy ends. 'In essence', he says, 'life is not a microscopic but a half-microscopic thing, a cell, some millimetres or whatsoever, is always an open system. A cell can only survive because it takes air, or eats. It is again a kind of dissipative structure or closed dissipative structure.'[35] Not all dissipative structures are living systems. What distinguishes the living from the non-living? The answer is autopoiesis. The Chilean biologist Humberto Maturana proposed the term to describe the self-producing qualities of living systems and the phenomenon of cognition: 'a living system is an autonomous unity, self-assertive in its dynamic capacity to withstand deformation under continuous turnover of matter while remaining invariant in its organization'.[36] Our bodies are like self-generating machines made up of a collection of organs, tissue and billions of cells, each one of which has the capacity for independent life. They order complex series of interactions on the basis of internally produced predictions that these interactions will reproduce the same internal state. Living systems are alive, 'only while all their structural changes are structural changes that conserve their autopoiesis. That is, a living system dies when its autopoiesis stops being conserved through its structural changes'.[37]

Living systems, says Maturana, are cognitive because their interactions are inferential. Cognition, which in human beings includes consciousness, is the self-producing process of life. Unlike other living organisms, humans realise their living in language. In language, nature meets culture in what Maturana calls ' the recursive co-ordinations of behaviour'.[38] He uses the term 'bodyhood' to describe the corporeal coming together of biological life and cultural meaning. Bodyhood is the result of our living in language that began three million years ago. It is founded upon the innate and consensual emotional communication that belonged to humanity's 'non-languaging' ancestors. Contemporary language and relational behaviour remains interlaced with this flow of emotion. Maturana describes this intertwining of emotion and language as conversation. Humanness is the transgenerational conservation of conversations. 'Our emotions guide moment after moment our doings by specifying the relational domain in which we operate'. It is emotion, rather than rational behaviour, that specifies our human identity in a self-reproducing process: 'whatever configuration of conversations that begins to be conserved in our living, becomes henceforth the world that we live, or one of the worlds that we live.'[39]

Maturana's 'conversations' make worlds in much the same way as Heidegger's worldhood is given in language. The cognition of the biologist, founded in non-conceptual, pre-reflexive, intuition, echoes the attunement of the philosopher's Being. Schrodinger's short book did not break new ground, but in countering the reductive tendencies of science, it offers a different kind of story about the relationship of biological life to culture and politics. The work of Prigogine and Maturana reveals the interdependency of life forms. In a universe running down to a 'heat death', life persists as a dynamic, self-reproducing web of interconnection between living and non-living matter. This has been most clearly expressed in James Lovelock's metaphor of Gaia. The earth is a self regulating system in which life and its material environment are 'massively interconnected'.[40] It is best thought of as a superorganism. Life, says Lovelock, is a 'planetary scale phenomenon with a cosmological life span' (p39). The Earth's atmospheric edge to space marks the boundary of a living organism: 'there is no clear distinction anywhere on the earth's surface between living and non-living matter' (p39).

Science is offering new understandings of living processes which might consign to history the ancient distinction between *zoe* and *bios*. A new relationship between biological life and political life is possible, but one which is not confined to human beings alone. It would include non-human living organisms as actors in political representation. Schrodinger concludes his book with his own philosophical speculation. He presents two suppositions:

> My body functions as a pure mechanism according to the Laws of Nature ...
> (ii) Yet I know, by incontrovertible direct experience, that I am directing its motions. The inference from these two fact is that 'I' control the 'motion of the atoms' according to the Laws of Nature.[41]

What is this 'I'? Each person imagines that an inventory of their memory and life experiences creates a coherent unit, distinct from any other person. But, Schrodinger suggests, close introspection reveals that it is not these individual traits that form the 'I', but the 'ground-stuff' on which they are collected. 'Ground stuff' is a vague term. It might be Aristotle's *zoe*, Heidegger's earth, Maturana's pre-linguistic intuiting, perhaps Freud's id. Each refers to a condition of living upon which consciousness, worldliness, the realm of freedom and individuality is formed. For Schrodinger it acquires a theological meaning. Each individual consciousness is formed from a larger whole. Like the Hindu Upanishads of 2500 years ago, in which the personal self equals the omnipresent, all-comprehending eternal self, science points to our union with 'all things'.

Individual consciousness lifts human beings from our materiality and enables us to escape from the realm of necessity. This historical process uproots us from the earth. In the modern world of post-industrial societies our bodies have become objects to be performed and managed as part of our cultural capital. Emotions come to be seen as arbitrary and destructive. The nature of our interdependency is obscured and disrupted by the practices of acquisitive individualism. Modern life and its artefacts effect a form of absence from 'living itself'. We fill this absence with sentimental attachments to the natural world and a morbid fear of death. Society exists in tandem to the environment, which becomes an object that requires working on, repair or 'saving'. But if we take Lovelock's metaphor seriously, human life cannot be separated off from the environment. We form a part of it, as much as the rocks, trees and grassland. Biological life separated from social life does violence to 'living itself'. But where the natural sciences seek theories that evoke universal laws, the social sciences must deal with historical contingency. History warns us that to bring together the biological and the social evokes blood and soil nationalism and its biological destiny of 'the race'. When it has been threatened, the ethnic nation state has retreated into the mysticism of prehistory. To transcend the distinction between biology and society means to reach beyond national community and racial difference toward a planetary dialogue about our collective fate.

Earthbound

In October 2004, two US environmental activists, Michael Shellenberger and Ted Nordhaus, presented a document, 'The Death of Environmentalism', to a meeting of the Environmental Grantmakers Association. The environmental movement, they claimed, had failed. 'Over the last fifteen years environmental foundations and organizations have invested hundreds of millions of dollars into combating global warming. We have strikingly little to show for it'.[42] They argued that the environmental movement's foundational concepts and institutions were outmoded. Why are some problems designated environmental while others are not? Why is global warming framed as an environmental problem but not poverty and war? The problem of global warming requires letting go of old identities, categories and assumptions. The prescriptive moralism of environmentalism – telling people what they can't have and can't do – needs to find a more aspirational politics that links together the economic, the social and the environmental in pursuit of a sustainable and more equitable life. In December, former Sierra Club President Adam Werbach repeated Shellenberger's and Nordhaus's message at San Francisco's Commonwealth Club: 'I say to you tonight … Environmentalism is dead'.[43] Environmentalism cannot deal with the most pressing ecological challenges. 'If humans are part of the environment, then how can some human problems be "environmental" and others not?' (p16). For Werbach, the concept of our interconnectedness has been lost. The task of ecological politics is not to simply protect things like trees and parks, but to persuade people to recognise the collective interdependence of humanity.

To be earthbound is 'to be held to', and 'to be in common with', the natural world. To be earthbound does not involve going in search of the blood and soil of one's exclusive national or racial destiny; nor does it involve a nostalgic return to the past, or subjection to the raw vicissitudes of nature. It is not about rejecting the cultures of urban life and returning to cultivating the land. It is about the ethical experience of becoming who we are in connectedness to the living and non-living systems that have created us. Individuals are not born free. We make ourselves free, and we do so not in isolation from others but in relation to them, and in relation to the plants and animals that sustain us. Climate change has reframed necessity. It is no longer confined to the realm of the private household, nor solely located in the naked life of the stateless and the excluded. It has broken free of political sovereignty because it can no longer be assimilated into the nation state and the national polity. It encompasses earthly life itself. The collective future of humanity has been brought into question. The gross inequalities of the world belie the idea that all humanity will share the same fate, but the wealthy populations will not escape unscathed. Our consumer societies have come to fear nature as the death which awaits us. Death has been cloaked in technology and hidden away in hospital wards. To become earthbound is to accept mortality, finitude and limitation into our lives. There is no ultimate freedom from necessity. We are free only so far as our dependency on others, both living and non-living entities, enables us to be free. We require much more than just our individual lives to secure ourselves against entropy.

NOTES

1. Hannah Arendt, *The Human Condition*, University of Chicago Press 1998, p5.
2. Buzz Aldrin, address to the joint session of Congress, 16.9.69, www.hq.nasa.gov/office/pao/History/ap11ann/comments.htm.
3. Peter Schwartz, Doug Randall, *An Abrupt Climate Change Scenario and Its Implications for United States Security*, 2003, www.ems.org/climate/pentagon_climate_change.html.
4. David Stipp, 'The Pentagon's Weather Nightmare', *Fortune*, 9 February 2004, www.fortune.com/fortune/technology/articles/0,15114,582584,00.html.
5. Mark Townsend, Paul Harris, 'Now the Pentagon tells Bush: climate change will destroy us', *The Observer*, 22.2.04, http://observer.guardian.co.uk/international/story/0,6903,1153513,00.html.
6. For a debate about climate conflict see: Ragnhild Nordås & Nils Petter Gleditsch, 'Climate Conflict: Common Sense or Nonsense?', Department of Sociology and Political Science, Norwegian University of Science and Technology NTNU; International Peace Research Institute, Oslo 2005, www.statsvitenskap.uio.no/konferanser/nfkis/cr/Nordas.pdf.
7. *Special Report on Emissions Scenarios*, IPCC, 2000, http://sres.ciesin.org/.
8. *Climate Change 2001: Impacts, Adaptation, and Vulnerability*, Working Group 11, IPCC 2001, p3, www.ipcc.ch/pub/wg2SPMfinal.pdf.
9. *Change 2001: Synthesis Report*, 'Summary for Policy Makers', IPCC 2001, p5, www.ipcc.ch/pub/spm22-01.pdf.
10. *Impacts, Adaptation, and Vulnerability*, 2001, p3, op cit; Synthesis Report, 2001, p6, ibid.
11. *Synthesis Report*, ibid, pp14-15.
12. Peter A. Stott, D.A. Stone, M.R. Allen, 'Human contribution to the European heatwave of 2003', *Nature*, Vol. 432, 2.12.04.

13. *World Energy Outlook 2004*, International Energy Agency, 2004, p29, www.iea.org/textbase/publications/free_new_Desc.asp?PUBS_ID=1266.

14. International Scientific Steering Committee, *International Symposium on the Stabilisation of greenhouse gas concentrations*, Hadley Centre, Exeter, UK, February 2005, May 2005, p5, www.stabilisation2005.com/Steering_Commitee_Report.pdf.

15. C.G. Rapley, 'Antarctic Ice Sheet and Sea Level Rise', presentation to the International Symposium on the Stabilisation of greenhouse gas concentrations, www.stabilisation2005.com/programme.html.

16. Earth Observatory, 'Record Low for June Arctic Sea Ice', June 2005, http://earthobservatory.nasa.gov/Newsroom/NewImages/images.php3?img_id=16978. See also national snow and ice data centre, http://nsidc.org/.

17. Hadley Centre, *Stabilising climate to avoid dangerous climate change – a summary of relevant research at the Hadley Centre*, January 2005, Department for Environment, Food and Rural Affairs, p8, www.metoffice.com/research/hadleycentre/pubs/brochures/.

18. Tonje Folkestad, Mark New, Jed O. Kaplan, Josefino C. Comiso, Sheila Watt-Cloutier, Terry Fenge, Paul Crowley, Lynn D. Rosentrater, *Evidence and Implications of Dangerous Climate Change in the Arctic*, www.stabilisation2005.com/37_Tonje_Folkestad.pdf

19. Jonathan Leake, 'Britain faces big chill as ocean current slows', *The Times*, 8 May 2005, www.timesonline.co.uk/article/0,,2087-1602579,00.html.

20. Carl Wunsch, 'What is the Thermohaline Circulation?', *Science*, Vol. 298, 8 November 2002, http://puddle.mit.edu/~cwunsch/.

21. Bogi Hansen, Svein Osterhus, Detlef Quadfasel, William Turrell, 'Already the Day After Tomorrow?', *Science*, Vol 305, Issue 5686, 953-954, 13 August 2004, www.sciencemag.org/cgi/content/summary/305/5686/953?rbfvr Token=4fbb65d6416844d6efc896cae6ec245e95a48a0e.

22. Hadley Centre, *Stabilising climate to avoid dangerous climate change – a summary of relevant research at the Hadley Centre*, op cit, p5.

23. Michael E. Schlesinger, Jianjun Yin, Gary Yohe, Natalia G. Andronova, Sergey Malyshev, Bin Li, *Assessing the Risk of a Collapse of the Atlantic Thermohaline Circulation*, www.stabilisation2005.com/Schlesingerm_Thermohaline.pdf. For a detailed debate on this issue see, www.realclimate.org/index.php?p=159.

24. Hadley Centre, *Stabilising climate to avoid dangerous climate change – a summary of relevant research at the Hadley Centre*, op cit, p7.

25. John Pickrell, 'Soil may spoil UK's climate efforts', *New Scientist*, 7.9.05, www.newscientist.com/article.ns?id=dn7964.

26. John Vidal, 'CO2 rise threatens Britain's hope of meeting the Kyoto target', *The Guardian*, 5.9.05.

27. William Wordsworth, 'Lines Composed a Few Miles Above Tintern Abbey', 1798, *William Wordsworth Favourite Poems*, Dover Publications 1992.

28. Klaus Eder, *The New Politics of Class Social Movements and Cultural Dynamics in Advanced Societies*, Sage 1993, ch 7.

29. Aristotle Ch.1, section 5, *Nicomachaen Ethics*, http://classics.mit.edu/Aristotle/nicomachaen.1.i.html.

30. Walter Benjamin, 'Critique of Violence', *One Way Street and Other Writings*, trans. Edmund Jephcott, Kingsley Shorter, Verso 1985, p151.

31. Giorgio Agamben, 'Form-of-Life', *Means without End*, University of Minnesota Press 2000, p4.

32. Martin Heidegger, 'The Origin of the Work of Art', *Poetry, Language, Thought*, trans. Albert Hofstadter, Harper & Row 1975, pp44-45.

33. Erwin Schrodinger, *What is life?*, http://home.att.net/~p.caimi/schrodinger.html.

34. Ibid.

35. Scientecmatrix.com, 'Getting to know Ilya Prigogine', ww.edu365.com/aulanet/comsoc/noticies/Complexity_IlyaPrigogine_interview.htm

36. Humberto Maturana, 'Autopoietic Organization', www.gwu.edu/ per cent7Easc/biographies/Maturana/SYMB/matauto.html.

37. Humberto Maturana, *Metadesign*, www.inteco.cl/articulos/metadesign_parte1.htm.

38. Ibid.

39. Ibid.

40. James Lovelock, *The Ages of Gaia*, Oxford University Press 2000, pxiii.

41. Erwin Schrodinger, *What is life?*, op cit.

42. Michael Shellenberger, Ted Nordhaus, *The Death of Environmentalism: Global Warming Politics in a Post-environmental World*, 2004, p6, http://www.thebreakthrough.org/.

43. Adam Werbach, '*Is Environmentalism Dead?*', 2004, p3, www.3nov.com/.

six | The future is ageing

My local post office is situated at the rear of a shop selling clothes. The queue of people extended past rows of cheap trousers and synthetic blouses. An old man wearing an Arsenal hat faded to pink gruffly shouted to the woman next in line, 'You're next. Go on!' After his outburst he stood there, lost in himself, his trousers hung loosely from his hips looking as empty as the trousers hanging on the rails. When he walked up to the counter he pushed through his book and said belligerently to the man behind the glass, 'don't ask me how I am today. I'm ill!' After I'd posted my package and left the post office, I glanced around to see if he might be outside Tesco sitting on one of the benches, or waiting for the bus. There was no sign of him. I thought, one day soon he would be dead – he had looked already lost to the underworld – and no-one would be any the wiser that his life had ended. He was an old man cast adrift from society.

The old have occupied a twilight zone of non-identity, reduced to the singular, asexual description of old: old codger, old biddy, old git, old bag. They become an embarrassment to the optimistic glow and aspirations of consumer culture. Ageing is a form of internal exile which precipitates a process of becoming anonymous. The old share the same street, live in the same block of flats, but they merge unnoticed into the hinterland of our gaze. As Sue Gerhardt writes, 'We have to be seen in order to exist as a self, and we are dependent on what others see, and how much of our "being" they recognise'.[1] Deprived of recognition, the old suffer the same silence and invisibility that surrounds the dying. The exclusion of the old from the world leaves the young to fill the absence with their own unspoken anxieties about what awaits them in their later years: the living death of loneliness without family and friends; fear of crime and strangers isolating one behind multi-bolted doors; daily shopping trips, visits to Accident and Emergency, the doctor's surgery, the launderette, for a short reprieve from the silence and the companionless noise of the television; the onset of Alzheimer's disease and a living decay of the self; cancer and a terrible death.

The terror of ageing is incarnated in the care home with its day room of arm-chaired, vacant-eyed men and women whose despair, powerlessness and boredom sap their will to live. As one paramedic reports on his BLOG Random Acts of Reality: 'I only tend to see the bad nursing homes. I'm not talking about nursing homes where the patients are abused in the tradition-al sense, but rather where they seem to have simply been ... left. I went to one the other day, run by a large prestigious private healthcare company, it is clean and looks very pretty. But I'd rather die than spend my final days there.'[2] Abuse in care homes, says the Royal College of Psychiatrists, is 'a common part of institutional life'.[3] The House of Commons Health Committee report on Elder Abuse cites a survey of community and district nurses in which 88 per cent of respondents encountered elder abuse at work.[4] The committee reckoned on a 'half a million older people abused at any one time'. Witnesses to the committee suggest that the figure is an underestimate. Awareness of the problem is growing, and so the rates of detection and reporting will increase (p11). Elder abuse is no longer just the obvious pushing, slapping, hitting, shouting, stealing-money kind. It involves the winnowing away of life through the over-medication of drugs, the institutionalised deprivation of sensory feeling, environments that generate emotional neglect and intellectual impoverishment, the abandon-ment to one's own lost existence in a nicely carpeted room.

Excluded from society, the old enter the past, which becomes charged with meaning. Memories recover an identity that has been lost, they dispel the fear of being forgotten. Meanwhile, in present time, subjected to the impotence of a second childhood, the old must endure the patronising condescension and indifference of society. Pensioned off and their labour power de-commodified, men and women are calculated to be economically without use or value. The old age pensioner is a category of welfare legislation, and this has reduced individuals to figures of frailty and dependency. In the UK, Help the Aged report that, in 2005, 2 million older people lived in poverty. The basic state pension of £82.05 a week for a single person and £131.20 for a couple is below the official poverty line, and a considerable shortfall on the budget necessary for basic requirements.[5] In consequence, over the last five years in England and Wales, between 20,000 and 50,000 people aged 65 and over have suffered avoidable winter deaths.[6]

Brush the caricatures aside – endearing grannies, dirty old men, dotty, shock-haired professors, tight-lipped shockable spinsters – and the old become the harbingers of our mortality. The failing body and growing dependency on others are an unwelcome reminder that our belief in being the artists of our own lives is, in the longer term, a conceit. Old age, like death itself, is an affront to the forward march of modernity and our desire to make something of our lives. Ignore it, avoid it, remove it from daily life, our strategies share a similar denial of its presence. Statistically speaking, we are likely to succumb to a chronic illness and end our life in a hospital, in an impersonal, possibly painful, techno-medical death. The exact character of this death, and the old age that precedes it, will be largely shaped by our economic status and the class we were born into. But this fate – the lack of hospice care, the minimal understanding of palliative medicine, the lack of opportunity to die at home – is also the political consequence of our collective evasion of our mortality, and the failure to accord integrity to ageing. The future in capitalist society must always be full of opportunity and better days. To be successful, individuals must manage their bodies and emotions to optimum, status-enhancing effect. To become old and succumb to biological destiny is to face eviction from the status-making game of consumption. Gendered performances fail. Diminishing prowess and the loss of appearance reduce individuals to insignificance. The old cease to count.

Market opportunities

In our corporate-dominated society, the desire to stem the advance of ageing has been transformed into a market opportunity for youth-enhancing, status-maintaining products. The global market in skin care is worth over £20 billion, a growing volume of which is for anti-ageing creams and moisturisers. Olay, which claims 19 per cent of the UK's £478m market, promotes its anti-ageing products with its '7 Rules of Anti-Ageing' – a regime of diet, intensive body management and mind exercises, combined with its anti-ageing moisturises and cleansing lotions.[7] Like its competitors, Olay relies on a bowdlerised version of science to legitimise its products: Regenerist, its 'next generation of anti-ageing skincare', harnesses 'an exclusive amino-peptide complex'.[8] The science is given credence by academics who sit on the industry's professional advisory boards or who work in corporate-sponsored research projects. The expanding market exploiting the plasticity of the body also includes the body modification industry. Its surgical interventions suction out unsightly subcutaneous fat, cut and tuck sagging breasts, buttocks and stomachs, tighten bags beneath the eyes, eradicate wrinkles and stretch loose skin around the throat. The desire for youth, like the gaze of Narcissus, can only see its own reflection. The political impotence and protracted economic dependency of the young, and the sheer difficulty of growing up, are nowhere acknowledged in the marketing spectacle of their fun-loving, sexualised bodies. Selling the illusion of youthful vigour, to stave off the psychological pain of the anonymity of ageing, is big business.

The commodification of the older body is part of the broader development of significant new markets servicing the older population and in the process inventing new identities, images and vocabularies of ageing. Business is exploiting the growing desire to live our longer lives more fully. 'Think Again', say the holiday firm Saga. Their brochure exhorts the older consumer to have 'no regrets': 'It's not always the things we have done that we regret – sometimes it's the things that we haven't done.' On the cover a silver-haired couple tango on a bleached white beach. Inside, another couple ride an elephant down a jungle-bound river. These are images of the 'new vision of later life'. According to HSBC bank, 'people increasingly see retirement and later life as a time of reinvention and an "opportunity for a whole new chapter in life"'.[9] HSBC offer the financial means to achieve this goal. The October 2005 issue of *Fortune* magazine introduces the guru of this cultural revolution in ageing: 'Ken Dychtwald has a message for ageing boomers and the corporations that sell to them: Retirement as we know it is over.'[10] Dychtwald has popularised the gerontologists' message of a longevity revolution. Global fertility rates are declining and people are living longer. 'From where I sit this longevity revolution will have a bigger impact on people's lives, their money, on the economy, on our families, on work, than either the industrial or technological revolutions of previous centuries.' The new old will reject the decline into anonymity and invisibility. They will be revitalised, health conscious and preoccupied with personal growth. The 'golden years of retirement' pottering around the home or golf course will be replaced by a new 25-30-year life stage of meaningful activity. Dychtwald's market research for investment bank Merrill Lynch claims that 'boomers indicate that today's linear life plan of distinct years for education, work and leisure is becoming obsolete. In its place is emerging a cyclic and phased life plan in which education, work and leisure exist in different proportions throughout life.'[11] Some will seek part-time work, while a significant minority will want to move in and out of work and leisure. A few will start their own business. They will be a living rebuttal of the spent lives of their parents' last years.

Dychtwald's vanguard in this revolution is the 78 million strong US baby-boom generation, who were born between 1946 and 1964. This 50-plus age group, which represents 27 per cent of the American population, earns $2 trillion a year and controls 70 per cent of the country's total wealth and 77 per cent of total assets. It is the grey dollar, and the financial services industries are targeting its massive wealth. 'Don't flunk retirement' cautions

Merrill Lynch. Investments are no longer enough. Planning for the new retirement will need a financial adviser: 'Meeting all the needs of this new way of living and retiring requires new advice that considers every aspect of your financial life'.[12] The accumulated wealth of the ageing is bringing into existence new services markets selling pension funds, investment schemes, specially tailored holidays and leisure activities, personal, institutional and health care. The global opportunities for trade in these services are considerable. The demographic revolution is not confined to the industrialised countries. The twenty-first century began with 600 million older people; by mid-century the number will be 2 billion.[13] On current projections, one in three individuals alive in 2150 will be aged over sixty.[14] The population division of the United Nations reports that 'the trend towards older populations is largely irreversible, with the young populations of the past unlikely to occur again'.[15] Business is recognising the profitable opportunities of the emerging cultural revolution in ageing. The old images of ageing – the fateful retreat from society, house slippers and waiting for the inevitable end – is giving way to representations of active, pleasure-seeking, potential-fulfilling individuals embarking on their third or fourth age. Prejudices against the old will increasingly be challenged. Ageism in the labour market will be outlawed as the working age population shrinks and the retirement age is raised.

The cultural revolution in ageing is an historic opportunity to begin living another stage of life. But beneath the growing abundance of promotional gloss and media hype, the future of ageing for the world majority is destined to be a time of financial insecurity, exclusion and poverty. Dychtwald, following the practice of fellow corporate evangelists, has taken a social trend and out of it spun a gospel of hope and optimism in service to capital accumulation. In 2000, the global support ratio of workers aged 15-64 to each person aged over 65 was 9:1. By 2050 it is expected to be 4:1.[16] In poorer countries the burden of the aged on a declining working population will intensify multiple forms of deprivation. According to the World Bank, 38 per cent of the ageing population in Mexico lives below the poverty line. Fidel Herrera Beltrin, governor of

Veracruz, reported that in his state 240,000 adults over seventy receive no social assistance.[17] In contrast, the ageing wealthy of the industrialised countries will create a demand for cheap, low-paid carers imported from the countries that are most at risk from the new demographics. The commodification and export of female care will cause destruction to family life and the care of children and the old. The cultural revolution in ageing is currently being dominated by the pursuit of profitable new markets. These will make no recompense for global poverty, nor will they alleviate the inequalities within rich countries. In 2001, the United States median net worth of older white households was $205,000 dollars; the median net worth of older black households was $41000.[18] In the UK the wealthiest 20 per cent of pensioners have an occupational pension and receive on average 82 per cent of average earnings. The poorest 20 per cent of pensioners, with only the basic state pension, receive 21 per cent of average earnings.[19] The good life that awaits the baby boom generation will be affordable only to those who can pay for it, or to those who can continue working in the new, deregulated, minimum wage, oldsters' labour market.

'Successful ageing' and pension reform

The new corporate ideology of 'successful ageing' encourages an individualised response to the process of growing older. Manage your body, take responsibility for your health and invest for your retirement and the future will be 'forever young'. This ignores the social deprivations and economic inequalities that make this kind of personal self-help regime impossible for the great majority of the world's population. Corporate interest in ageing is not motivated by a concern with the equitable well being of the older population. It is a political project that seeks to extend the role of the market into the later years of life and to do so by dismantling publicly provided pensions and services and transferring their profitable parts, and the tax revenues that pay for them, to private business.

President Bush has described his plans for a new pension scheme as the making of an 'ownership society' – 'if you own something, you have a vital stake in the future of our country'.[20] The Cato Institute, whose Wall Street financed Project on Social Security Privatisation has been spearheading the efforts to convert Social Security into a system of personal accounts, summarises its ethos: 'In the "ownership society", patients control their own health care, parents control their own children's education, and workers control their retirement savings.'[21] The pensions debate has been dominated by these vested interests, who stand to make substantial profits out of privatisation and who promote the myth that corporate-managed, individual savings accounts will improve freedom of choice and enhance wealth in old age. The Social Security programme, limited though it already is, has been the target of a relentless campaign by the Bush administration and its neo-conservative allies, who want to privatise it and hand it over to corporate providers. The aim is to sell off the programme's huge holdings of Treasury Bonds, with the proceeds being invested in the stock market. The more profitable individual retirement accounts would then be managed by brokerage houses, banks and mutual funds, who would charge fees ranging from 0.2 per cent to 1.4 per cent a year. (On average such fees can reduce pension lump sums by up to 30 per cent on retirement.) The majority of accounts would be unprofitable and managed by a burgeoning government bureaucracy.

Reform of the State Pension has also been a central feature of neo-liberal economic policy-making in Britain. Tony Blair has endorsed Bush's 'ownership society', describing the ownership of personal assets as the essential means necessary for escaping poverty and 'encouraging self-esteem and healthy habits of behaviour'.[22] The New Labour government's Pensions Commission, chaired by Adair Turner, vice-chairman of Merrill Lynch Europe, reported in 2006. His remit, he explained, did not involve improving the public pensions system. It was to consider the efficacy of compulsory private pensions.[23] While Tony Blair has favoured the financial industries as managers of individual savings accounts, the Commission came out in support of a publicly managed National Pensions Savings Scheme. The subsequent government White Paper on pensions evades making a decision and leaves open the question of who will manage the new pensions funds.

To understand the forces at work determining the future shape of the British pension system we need to look at market-based pensions reform in the past, not only in Britain but in the recent history of the economy of Chile, where it began. Behind the rhetoric of individual liberty and the 'ownership society', the future of ageing has been taking shape, fashioned around the interests of finance capital. Pension funding is about who gets to claim future surpluses of capital. It is about increasing the availability of relatively inexpensive older labour by raising the retirement age. Reform has involved redistributing public assets from labour to capital and from the poor to the rich. Until recently, the issue of pensions has been dismissed as the arcane concern of actuaries, civil servants and financial risk managers. But there is now a growing consciousness that the kind of provision government makes for pensions will shape the nature of our society. As Richard Minns argues, 'the privatisation of pensions is about the nature of total economic structure, not about pensions'.[24] The history of pension reform proves his point.

A brief history of pension reform

It begins in 1973 when the socialist government of Salvador Allende was overthrown in a military coup led by General Pinochet and engineered by the US. Within a few months the 'Chicago Boys' had taken over economic planning. Since the 1950s, groups of Chilean economists had been introduced to the teachings of Milton Friedman and Frederick von Hayek through an exchange programme between the University of Chicago and the Catholic University of Chile. In 1975 they initiated a 'radical austerity programme', opening up the economy to international trade and drastically reducing money supply and public spending. Traditional industry collapsed. At the same time capital markets were liberalised and strategic banks and industries privatised (sold off to a small oligopoly of rich Chilean families). The Chicago Boys' first phase of restructuring was supported by the IMF, in what can be seen as a forerunner of its later Structural

Adjustment Programmes. In 1980 a privately administered, national system of pension savings was introduced. Employers paid 10 per cent of their workers wages into individual savings accounts. (The army and police were exempt from this new system.) These were run as mutual funds by management companies known as Administradores de Fondos de Pensiones (AFPs). A 3 per cent charge was made against each account. The AFPs invested the workers' savings in the nascent stock and bond markets, creating a flow of pension funds into the newly liberalised and still immature capital markets. A speculative boom followed – with the state in the mean time shouldering the costs of the transition to the new system. This new pension scheme further intensified the concentration of assets amongst Chile's top families. When Chile's speculative bubble burst, as a result of high levels of borrowing in the economy, and the onset of the Latin American debt crisis, the value of the workers' pensions savings accounts was wiped out.[25]

The restructuring of the economy that followed included a further round of privatisations, and AFPs were offered for sale to foreign investors like Citicorp and the US health insurance company Aetna. Chile's business oligopoly used the revenue from the AFPs to buy stakes in the newly privatised industries and rebuild their empires in the wake of the debt crisis. The pension funds were used to help construct capital markets, but they were not used for investment: they were a means of transferring economic resources between companies and concentrating financial power. It was a classic example of Marx's observation that financial speculation is parasitic on labour. 'What the speculating trader risks is social property, not his own', writes Marx. 'Equally absurd now is the saying that the origin of capital is saving, since what this speculator demands is precisely that others should save for him'.[26] The reforms pioneered by the Chicago Boys had the net effect of eroding the value of employee pensions, but enriching a share-holding elite and those who owned the financial institutions. By 2004, according to Manuel Riesco of the Centro De Estudios Nacionales De Desarrollo Alternativo:

Today there is a wide consensus among experts that the Chilean private pension system will provide pensions on its own only to the upper income minority of the affiliates to the system. Even for them, it seems highly unsatisfactory, mainly because of the high fees charged by private pension administrators. These, in turn, are six companies that have become the most profitable Chilean industry, one that is immune to recessions, with average return on equity of over 50% a year since 1997. [27]

Riesco points out that 'public expenditure in pensions has remained consistently in the order of 6% of Chilean GDP since 1981'. However, the cost of the pension reform had been considerable: 'it has absorbed almost one-third of the overall government budget, and over 42% of public social expenditures'. [28] Despite this, according to Stephen Kay of the Federal Reserve Bank of Atlanta, 41 per cent of those eligible to collect pensions continue to work because of their poor value. [29] A worker retiring at the same time as a member of the military would receive less than half of the latter's pension.

Margaret Thatcher was a great supporter of General Pinochet, and an admirer of his neo-liberal programme. In her first budget in 1979 pensions were a target for reform. The aim, according to the Chancellor Geoffrey Howe, was 'to reduce the burden of financing the public sector, so as to leave commerce and industry to prosper'. [30] In future the statutory uprating of the pension would be based on the slower movement of prices and not on the movement of earnings. In 1986 the Conservatives introduced measures to reduce the level of the State Earnings Related Pension Scheme (SERPS), and individuals were encouraged to opt out of it, many of them into privately managed personal pension schemes. The problem with these schemes, however, was that there was no obligation on the providers, be they a life assurance company or a mutual fund, to ensure a reasonable income on retirement: the responsibility and risk lay solely with the individual pension owner. And as in Chile, this reform was heavily subsidised by the tax-payer, through the tax rebate incentives that were offered to those who opted out. But in spite of the huge amounts of government money spent on subsidising opting out, it was revealed in the subsequent mis-selling scandals that millions of the schemes that had been sold were manifestly ill suited for the individuals who had bought them. SERPS pensions that would have provided a reasonable income had been replaced by private schemes that would leave their owners impoverished in retirement. Once again the main effect of the reform had been to shift assets away from the state, and from employees, and into the hands of financial companies.

The iniquity and greed that were being exposed under the Conservatives' pension reform, and the drama of Chilean pensions, did not deter the authors of the influential 1994 World Bank report, *Averting the Old Age Crisis*.[31] The report promoted a 'multi-pillar' approach to pension reform. However it placed a heavy emphasis on only one of the pillars – a mandatory privately managed, individual defined contributions pension scheme. Chile's experiment was a model to emulate. In 1998, in a speech to the right-wing Heritage Foundation, the lead author, Estelle James, praised the Chilean reforms and the role of individual private pension plans in developing Chile's capital markets. Its system, she announced, 'has now spread throughout Latin America to Argentina, Mexico, Peru, Bolivia and Uruguay. It is going to sweep South America and is moving to Central America'.[32]

This model of pension reform did not go completely uncontested however. The following year Joseph Stiglitz, then Chief Economist at the World Bank, and Peter Orszag, an academic, gave a paper at the World Bank Conference, 'New Ideas About Old Age Security'. Dismissing privately managed individual savings accounts as a solution to the pensions problem, they stated: 'We have shown that most of the arguments in favour of this particular reform are based on a set of myths that are often not substantiated in either theory or practice'.[33]

The 'ownership society'

The privatisation of Chile's pensions developed its capital markets and provided an entry point for foreign finance companies into Latin America. Stephane Marguier, head of international sales at the French bank CDC Ixis Asset Management, makes this point in an interview: 'For us, Chile is a laboratory to experiment in Latin America'.[34] In Britain the Conservative pension reform had created a similar cavalier pursuit of economic advantage and profit. The cost of the mis-selling scandal was estimated at £13.5bn: £4bn compensation to priority cases, £7.5bn to younger victims and £2bn in administrative costs. The whole to be met by insurers and financial advisers.[35] However the Consumers Association claimed that the great majority of companies forced to pay compensation took the money from policyholders by underpaying the full returns on investment. The Association also claimed that £18bn in tax benefits had been wasted due to high management fees. In 2000, £500m was paid out in commission on with-profits savings bonds alone.[36] The average private pension fund was calculated to be worth £24000. On retirement it would generate an annual income of around £2500.[37] In 2004, 500,000 people abandoned private pensions and moved back into SERPS. The failure of the liberalisation of the pensions system has not damaged the careers of its architects and cheerleaders however. In the US, Estelle James was appointed to the President's Commission to Strengthen Social Security. She was still pronouncing on the benefits of the Chilean system in 2005, writing in the *Washington Post*, 'Has it been a success?' and answering with an emphatic 'Yes'.[38] Bush visited Chile in 2001 and told its then President Ricardo Lagos that: 'Congress could take some lessons from Chile, particularly when it comes to how to run our pension plans'.[39]

The mis-selling scandal is only one part of the unfolding debacle of neo-liberal pension reform in the UK. Geoffrey Howe's strategy has proved to be effective in terms of saving state money. The Ageing Working Group attached to the European Union's Economic Policy Committee reports that the UK's total ageing-related public spending in 2000 was one of the lowest in the EU at 17.4 per cent of GDP. This compares to Germany's 28.5 per cent and France's 26.5 per cent.[40] Despite the growing ageing population, the Working Group predicts that UK state expenditure on pensions will decline from 5.5 per cent of GDP in 2000 to 4.4 per cent of GDP in 2050 (p14). The subsequent White Paper on pensions makes no provision for a rise in state expenditure on pensions. This will mean a significant reduction in public expenditure, and compares with the European average of 10.4 per cent of GDP in 2000, rising to 13.3 per cent of GDP in 2050. Philip Davis of the UK Pension Institute calculates that the combined level of the state pension in 2000 amounted to 35 per cent of average earnings. He estimates that by 2040 they will have fallen to 25 per cent.[41] A proposed reform to SERPS that will change it from an earnings-related scheme to a flat rate payment will further reduce it to 20 per cent of average earnings (p11).

To date, the public provided British state pension is being phased out by stealth. The White Paper on pensions does not suggest a clear reversal of this process. It will re-establish the indexing of the state pension to earnings, but it will postpone this reform until 2012 at the earliest. Each year sees a decline in the relative value of the state pension further reducing pensioners' share of future national wealth. According to the government's own projections about a third of pensioners will still need to undergo means-testing in order to claim their full state entitlement.[42] Two million women face penury in retirement. The state pension was introduced in a post-war world in which women were expected to be economically dependent upon their husbands. To qualify for it requires thirty-five years of national insurance contributions. Women who have spent lives moving in and out of work or in part-time work, who have cared for children and older relatives, or who are divorced or widowed and are living alone, have not accumulated the necessary contributions and so have no entitlement to a pension. The White Paper provides no mechanism to qualify all older women for the basic state pension. Instead the contributing years needed to qualify have been reduced from 39 to 30.[43] In spite of being in the vanguard of the cultural revolution in ageing, the economic prospects of the baby boom generation are not good. A large proportion do not own the financial resources to fund an adequate pension for the future. Half the English population aged 50 or over have less than £12000 of financial assets and a quarter have less than £1500.[44] In 2003-04, two thirds of the UK population had incomes below the national average of £408 per week, a level of income that would return a derisory income from a defined contributions scheme.[45]

Neo-liberal pension reform seeks a fundamental shift of resources away from the state to private business and individuals. It has done this by reducing the value of the public provided state pension, introducing private managed individual savings accounts, and promoting defined contributions schemes in place of defined benefit schemes. The latter change is crucial because it shifts the financial risk away from business and onto the individual account holder. The shift has been spurred on by the underfunding and subsequent closure of growing numbers of defined benefit pension schemes run by individual companies. In May 2005, United Airlines won court permission to retract its contractual pension obligations. The US taxpayer, through the Pension Guarantee Corporation, will shoulder the cost. This follows similar action by Pan Am, TWA and US Airways.[46] In a highly competitive market, pension funds have become a serious burden. Cutting the benefits paid to employees gives a business an advantage over its competitors. In the UK, occupational pension schemes have been vital to the proper functioning of the pension system, but their collapse has been more precipitous than in the US. The CBI estimates that the occupational pension fund deficit is between £160 and £300bn.[47] Companies are seeking to minimise their obligations either by offering only defined contribution schemes, or by winding up their defined benefit schemes, or closing the door to new members.

To gain popular acceptance in democratic countries, neo-liberal pension reform has had to rely on the ideology of the 'ownership society' to secure its legitimacy. Two decades of economic liberalisation in the UK has created an 'ownership society' characterised by low wages, social insecurity and the demise of collective forms of welfare provision. The personal assets that are supposed to replace public pension provision are, for a large minority of the population, either non-existent or tenuous. 11.3 million workers make no contributions to an occupational pension scheme; 4.6 million have no assets for retirement.[48] The transfer of risk from business and the state to the individual means that personal freedom has a high price attached to it. Individual choice is compromised by the deepening of class inequalities and the creation of widespread indebtedness. Household indebtedness in the UK in September 2005 stood at £1.130.2bn, of which £190.7bn was consumer credit.[49] 53 per cent of families have unsecured debts, owing on average £7065.[50] The Citizens Advice Bureau reported 1.1 million debt enquiries in 2003.[51] Debt is the economic dynamo of the 'ownership society'. The aggressive selling of credit by the financial services industry has helped to boost consumer demand as a strategy for managing the global overproduction of goods. It has enabled individuals in the US and UK to extend their purchasing of assets and commodities beyond the limits imposed by their personal income. However indebtedness has created indentured forms of consumption as increasing proportions of an individual's income is assigned to debt repayment. Like pension savings, debt establishes guaranteed flows of revenue that can facilitate the concentration of financial power and the accumulation of future surpluses. The ideological project of pension reform has been aimed at capturing long-term financial flows to private business for profit, by transferring public pension assets and tax revenues to the stock market. This fact is closer to the truth of the 'ownership society' than the folksy images of leisured old age promoted by the private pension providers.

The ending

A lead feature in the *Observer* in October 2005 was headed 'The third-agers': 'In today's Britain, people are no longer growing old quietly … we bring together an inspiring group of over-seventies for whom "retirement" is a dirty word'.[52] A fortnight later the cover of *Newsweek* proclaimed: 'Ready or not BOOMERS turn 60'. Inside, J. Walker Smith of polling company Yankelovich is quoted as saying, 'Baby boomers think they're going to die before they get old'. 'Let's face it', writes Norbert Bobbio at eighty five, contradicting these media eulogies for old age, 'it is impossible to ignore the fact that old people are increasingly marginalised in an age marked by the faster and faster pace of historical change'.[53] In traditional societies the old embodied cultural heritage. They passed on the rules, morals and customs that governed community and family life. Modernity has tipped the hierarchy of age upside down. The old are no longer in the know. New technologies transform the media and means of communication. Mores and values shift and slide. The old are custodians of nothing but their own memories. Onto the cultural blank screen of ageing the media and promotional culture paste the promise of psychological youth. Commerce sings its eulogies, promising a cornucopia of leisure and consumption. Old age will be a bounteous unfolding of new experience. Life begins at 50 ... 60 ... 70. 'Take control of your own future' exhorts the October 2005 issue of *Fortune* magazine. How should we achieve this? 'RETIRE RICH – Save Smarter, Build the Perfect Portfolio, Supercharge your IRA, Find your Personal Paradise: 5 Exotic Overseas Bargains.' In its clamorous pursuit of selling us an old age, capitalism irons out the density, contradictions and variety of human experience. It ignores those who can't afford it and generates an hysterical denial of decline, infirmity, diminishment, and death for those who can.

The cultural revolution in ageing marks a new phase of capital accumulation. It is giving rise to a new politics of ageing, in which the struggle for equality and economic justice against corporate capital will be central. How might we give new kinds of meaning to the cultural revolution in ageing? Not by denying death and decline, nor by suffering the ersatz life of the commercial market. We will need to give political expression to ageing. The lack of political power exposes the ageing to a state of non-living. Bobbio cites the medical technology which not so much keeps the old alive but prevents them from dying – 'You don't continue to live, you just can't die'. He describes his own old age as a long descent into the void – 'much longer than I would have ever imagined':

> I would say that mine is a melancholic old age, and by melancholy I mean the awareness of what has not been achieved and what is no longer achievable. It corresponds to the view of life as a road, along which the destination constantly shifts further down, and as soon as you reach it, you realise that it is not the final destination you first thought. Old age is the moment when you become fully aware that not only have you not finished your journey, but you will also never have the time to do so (p14).

Life can only be incomplete. Dreams will invariably be unrealised. Living ends in a failing of desire. Such sentiments are the nightmare of consumer culture, which responds to mortality with embarrassed silence. Ideas about death have traditionally been expressed in religious language, but they require a secular voice which can give value to being alive in the only world we will know. The lasting satisfactions of Bobbio's life were not his fame or intellectual achievements but his relationships with other people: 'everyone I have loved or who has loved me, and everyone who has been close to me' (p30). I return to the old man in the post office and the reason why I went looking for him after I had posted my package. I think it was because he was a man who appeared to be without friends. Who would bear witness to his life?

NOTES

1. Sue Gerhardt, 'The myth of self creation', *British Journal of Psychotherapy*, Vol. 17, No.3, Spring 2001, p340.

2. Random Acts of Reality, http://randomreality.blogware.com/, 2005.

3. Royal College of Psychiatrists, *Council Report CR84 Institutional Abuse of Older Adults*, June 2000, p6, www.rcpsych.ac.uk/publications/cr/cr84.htm.

4. House of Commons Health Committee, *Elder Abuse Second Report of Session 2003-04 Volume 1*, 2004, www.publications.parliament.uk/pa/cm200304/cmselect/cmhealth/111/111.pdf, p11.

5. Help the Aged, 'Poverty', 2005 www.helptheaged.org.uk/CampaignsNews /Poverty/_default.htm; for calculations, see the Family Budget Unit, budget www.york.ac.uk/res/fbu/publications.htm.

6. Help the Aged, op cit.

7. Pat Thomas, 'Behind the Label Skin Cream', *The Ecologist*, March 2005, www.theecologist.org/archive_detail.asp?content_id=379.

8. Olay, 'The 7 Rules of Anti-Ageing', 2005, www.olay.co.uk/newsandsamples /total-effects/7rules.jsp; http://www.olay.co.uk/regenerist/products.jsp.

9. HSBC, *The Future of Retirement*, 2005, www.hsbc.com/public/groupsite/ retirement_future/en/_overview_future_of_retirement.jhtml.

10. Nicholas Varchaver, 'Pitchman for the Gray Revolution', *Fortune*, October 2005, www.agewave.com/media.shtml#fortune.

11. Merrill Lynch, 'Living Younger Longer', The New Retirement Survey 2005, http://askmerrill.ml.com/html/mlrr_learn_living/.

12. Merrill Lynch, 'The New Retirement Calls for New Advice. It's time for

Total Merrill', 2005, Advice http://askmerrill.ml.com/html/mlrr_learn_advice/.

13. United Nations Department of Economic and Social Affairs (UNDESA), 'Executive Summary', *World Population Ageing: 1950-2050*, 2002, pxxix, ww.un.org/esa/population/publications/worldageing19502050/index.htm.

14. United Nations Department of Social and Economic Affairs, 'The Ageing of the World's Population', 2003, www.un.org/esa/socdev/ageing/ageing/agewpop.htm.

15. UNDESA, *World Population Ageing: 1950-2050*, op cit.

16. Ibid.

17. Globalaging.org, 'Mexico: The World Bank Reports a 38% Poverty Rate Among Mexico's Elderly', September 2005; 'Mexico: Fidel Provides Benefits for Elderly', October 2005, www.globalaging.org/pension/world/.

18. Federal Interagency Forum on Aging Related Statistics, 'New Release Federal Forum Reports Americans Aging Well, But Gaps Remain', 2004, p2, www.agingstats.gov/chartbook2004/pr2004.html.

19. E. Philip Davis, *Is there a Pension Crisis in the UK? Discussion Paper PI-0401*, Pensions Institute, March 2004, p9, www.pensions-institute.org/.

20. George Bush, 2004, www.whitehouse.gov/news/releases/2004/08/20040809-9.html.

21. The Cato Institute, 'The Ownership Society', 2005, www.cato.org/special/ownership_society/index.html.

22. David Boaz, 'Defining an Ownership Society', The Cato Institute 2003, www.cato.org/special/ownership_society/boaz.html.

23. Adair Turner, speech to the CBI Pensions Conference, 17 October 2003, www.pensionscommission.org.uk/publications/index.asp.

24. Richard Minns, 'Pensions of Mass Destruction', *Soundings 24*, Autumn 2003, p56.

25. Details of Chile's transition to a private pensions scheme came from: Greg Anrig Jr, 'No Way, José', The Century Foundation, December 2004, ww.tcf.org/list.asp?type=NC&pubid=799; Daniel Brandt, 'US Responsibility for the Coup in Chile', November 1998, www.namebase.org/chile.html; funds-europe, 'Cross-Border Explorer – Chile', May 2003, www.funds-europe.com/p_Headline.cfm?id=74; Manuel Riesco, 'The Chilean Pension System, A Quarter Century On', 2004, Centro de Estudios Nacionales de Desarrollo Alternativo, http://cep.cl/; S. Rosenfeld and J. L. Marre, *Chile's Rich*, *NACLA Report on the Americas*, May/June 1997, www.hartford-hwp.com/

archives/42a/100.html.

26. The quote is from Volume 3 of Karl Marx's *Capital* and was taken from Doug Henwood, 'Pension fund socialism: the illusion that just won't die', 2004, www.leftbusinessobserver.com/NSPensions.html.

27. Manuel Riesco, *The Chilean Pension System, A Quarter Century On*, Centro de Estudios Nacionales de Desarrollo Alternativo, 2004, http://cep.cl/.

28. Ibid.

29. Stephen J. Kay, *State Capacity and Pensions*, Research Department, Federal Reserve Bank of Atlanta, 2003, p12, www.frbatlanta.org/filelegacydocs/StateCapacityandPensionsKay.pdf.

30. Geoffrey Howe, 1979 Budget Speech, www.margaretthatcher.org/archive/displaydocument.asp?docid=109497.

31. The World Bank, *Averting the Old Age Crisis*, 1994, www-ds.worldbank.org/servlet/WDS_IBank_Servlet?pcont=details&eid= 000009265_3970311123336.

32. Estelle James, 'Social Security Reform, Lessons From Other Nations', speech delivered at the Heritage Foundation, 9 April 1998, p4, www.estelle james.com.

33. Peter R. Orszag and Joseph E. Stiglitz, 'Rethinking Pension Reform: Ten Myths About Social Security Systems', World Bank Conference, New Ideas About Old Age Security, September 14-15, 1999, p38, www.worldbank.org/knowledge/chiefecon/conferen/papers/rethinking.pdf.

34. funds europe, *Cross Border Explorer – Chile*, May, 2003, www.funds-europe.com/p_Headline.cfm?id=74.

35. Rupert Jones, 'Mis-selling bill tops £13bn', *The Guardian*, 2 December 2000, http://money.guardian.co.uk/pensionsmisselling/story/0,1456,594876,00.html.

36. Patrick Collinson, 'Insurers duck mis-selling bill', *The Guardian*, 7 February 2001, http://money.guardian.co.uk/pensionsmisselling/story/0,1456,595241,00.html.

37. International Longevity Centre-UK, *Funding the New Longevity Pensions*, Appendix 2, www.ilcuk.org.uk/publications.cfm.

38. Estelle James, 'How It's Done in Chile', *Washington Post*, 13 February 2005, www.washingtonpost.com/wp-dyn/articles/A18478-2005Feb12.html.

39. The Cato Institute, 'Bush Says Chile Has Lessons for U.S. on Social

Security', 23 April 2001, www.socialsecurity.org/daily/04-23-01.html.

40. Economic Policy Committee Working Group on Ageing Population, *The impact of ageing populations on public finances: overview of analysis carried out at EU level and proposals for a future work programme*, 2003, p6, http://europa.eu.int/comm/economy_finance/epc/epc_ageing_en.htm.

41. E. Philip David, op cit, p11.

42. Information about the implications of the Government's White Paper on pensions comes from a paper by Robin Blackburn 'Pensions – Meaningful Controversy – not Hollow Consensus', which was submitted to the Compass Manifesto working party on political economy, May/June, 2006. For his work on pensions see his book *Banking on Death*, Verso 2005.

43. Ibid.

44. James Banks, Carl Emmerson, Zoe Oldfield, *Preparing for Retirement: The Pension Arrangements and Retirement Expectations of those Approaching State Pension Age in England*, Institute of Fiscal Studies 2005, p15, www.ifs.org.uk/publications.php?publication_id=3396.

45. The Institute of Fiscal Studies, *Poverty and Equality in Britain 2005*, Executive Summary, 2005, www.ifs.org.uk/comms/summ_comm99.pdf.

46. Bernard Wasow, 'Confronting New Realities on Pensions', The Social Security Network 2005, www.socsec.org/commentary.asp?opedid=1003.

47. CBI, 'Focus on investment: the impact of pension deficits', Economic Brief 2003, Confederation of British Industry, www.cbi.org.uk/ndbs/positiondoc. nsf/81e68789766d775d8025672a005601aa/54658f64b842495b80256d7b003 ba9f3?OpenDocument.

48. Financial Services Authority, *Financial Risk Outlook 2005*, 2005, p36, www.fsa.gov.uk/pubs/plan/ financial_risk_outlook_2005.pdf.

49. Bank of England 'Lending to Individuals September 2005', Table A, Table C, www.bankofengland.co.uk/statistics/li/current/index.htm.

50. Financial Services Authority, op cit, p41.

51. Citizens Advice Bureau, 'consumer debt problems rose by three quarters in last seven years latest figures show', 21 October 2004, www.citizensadvice.org.uk/mac/index/pressoffice/press_index/press-041020.htm.

52. Geraldine Bedell, 'The third-agers', Review, *Observer*, 30 October 2005, www.observer.guardian.co.uk/ review/story/0,6903,1604278,00.html.

53. Norbert Bobbio, *Old Age and other essays*, Polity 2001, p5.

Afterword

The central argument of this book is that we are a society of individuals. We are social beings born with the primary urge to relate, trust and cooperate. We bring into the world our own propensities, but our minds and our individuality are shaped by the cultures, values, conscious and unconscious communications we grow up within. In turn our efforts to create our own individualities shape society. 'Individualisation' is an historical development of the relationship of the individual and society, restructuring it and changing the meaning and character of both in the process. The resurgence of liberal market capitalism over the last three decades has accelerated the promotion of the 'me' over the 'we'. Today there exists a dispersed but pervasive insecurity; a sense that our affluent lives are finely balanced between security and precariousness. In gaining unprecedented levels of individual choice we have become disconnected from a common shared life. This loss of belonging has its antecedents in earlier periods of modernity. It can create the feelings of 'nullity' that Max Weber has described as 'disenchantment', and which Georg Simmel likened to the meaning of life slipping through our fingers.

Democracy has been the historical urge toward dialogue and understanding. The demand for political representation has inaugurated the emergence of new classes, groups and identities. It has been a demand for recognition which has contained within it an ethical impulse of reciprocity. Out of reciprocity comes a search for justice and belonging. Contemporary changes in individuality and society face us with fundamental questions about the vitality of this democratic impulse. How are we to live together not only as free and equal individuals in a multicultural society, but also as a species on earth? What kind of politics and political institutions do we need to create a sense of belonging in a just society of individuals?

The capacity of society to collectively ask itself these questions has been diminished by a loss of confidence in our democratic institutions. Political parties are outdated and bereft of any meaningful social function. What has become of 'the social' that defines us as 'individuals in common'? The anxiety of finding ourselves with strangers in a world that holds no intrinsic meaning or purpose requires an openness to others. A readiness to share the world, writes Hannah Arendt, is the precondition for 'humanity': 'We humanize what is going on in the world and in ourselves only by speaking of it, and in the course of speaking of it we learn to be human.' [1] Individuals seek this kind of meaning or 'point to life' in the paradoxical moment when they sense they are losing it. Meaning is not pre-existing and waiting to be rediscovered, it will have to be created out of the philosophical resources and traditions at people's disposal.

To avoid cruelty and injustice, we have no choice but to face one another and persevere in our efforts to make contact and establish communication. In this activity a group might form, and in this group a collective, political endeavour might evolve, and in this endeavour something of value might be created and each person be given recognition by the other. The common good which we can bring into social existence through political thought hinges on this capacity to grant each other recognition. The giving of recognition and the need to be recognised by others is fundamental to our existence. It confers self-esteem in which lies the wish for a good life in which others are esteemed. Mutual recognition of difference marks a respect for the integrity of others. Its absence through oppression, bad faith, exploitation, the utilisation of power in pursuit of self or sectional interest represents the dissolution of meaningfulness. Without meaning society cannot foster the conditions in which love will flourish. Love comes from others, and coming from others it infuses self love. The loss of the love of others by being assaulted, rejected, slighted, humiliated, demeaned, disrespected, ignored, diminishes love of the self and results in the state of shame. Shame is a mortification, a death of the self and where there is shame in those who suffer injustice, there will also be violence in an attempt to save the self.

There can be no after identity. Not literally. There is no end to identity, just as there is no end to language. The word after governs the word identity, preceding it in time and locating identity in the past where it takes on a more definable character. We analyse and understand what already belongs to the past. Identity in the present is much harder to grasp. It is passing, and in its passing something new, as yet unidentifiable, is emerging. We are always in the midst of language and we are always in the process of making identity. We can speak of identity, but its passage through time, its multiplication and difference, disperses its narrative coherence. Identity begins to lose its meaning and in losing meaning it ignites a search for new meaning. We struggle to occupy an identity in order to anchor ourselves in the world. It is the phonetics of our belonging. It demands our reflexivity – how we interact with our race, class, gender, age, religion – and it extends the realm of the ethical.

But faced with incommensurable disagreement it can trigger a counter reaction in attempts to fix identity and close it off from difference through exclusion and discrimination. For those who are powerless and disenfranchised, securing an identity which is free of ambiguity represents the achievement of self definition out of which springs collective action. But the apparent concreteness and sharply defined, closely policed borders of such singular identities make them vulnerable to implosion and collapse. The rigidity of their internal coherence bespeaks their weakness and their inability to carry the cause of justice beyond the hour of their own liberation. Such identities of security cannot be the basis for a politics of freedom and justice.

Dialogue and mutual recognition are the preconditions of justice and these require identities that face the open, and whose narratives can accommodate the presence of more than one voice. These are identities of reciprocity in which esteem is mutually given. To flourish they require the condition of equality which lies at the heart of justice. We are not born free, we make ourselves free. In freedom we must necessarily face difference and its incommensurability. What we have to confront is our own hatred and fear. We both act upon and are acted upon by others. A humanism without guarantees is simply a willingness to persevere in life in the knowledge that our self preservation is dependent upon our preservation of others. This ethic of reciprocity does not promise the individual an afterlife or a heaven on earth. Its gift is mortal, finite and contingent, but it is what makes us human.

NOTES

1. Hannah Arendt, 'On Humanity in Dark Times', *Men in Dark Times*, Pelican Books, 1973, p32.

Acknowledgements

Some of the essays first appeared in other publications, though they have been extensively revised for this book. 'Ghosts' appeared in Jo Littler and Roshi Naidoo (eds), *Ethnicity and Heritage*, Routledge 2005. It is reprinted by permission of Taylor and Francis. 'Fallen Among Thieves' was published in *Mediactive*, issue 4, Lawrence & Wishart 2005; 'At War' appeared in *Cultural Studies*, Vol. 19, No. 5, 2005. It is reprinted by permission of Taylor and Francis.

The book was written with the financial support of Middlesex University. The Arts & Humanities Research Council provided funding for a sabbatical through its research leave scheme. I would like to acknowledge the lecturers, group conductors and in particular the seminar participants at the Institute of Group Analysis, who over the last two years have been a significant influence in giving shape to the ideas in this book (www.groupanalysis.org). And lastly, thank you Paul, who was a part of the beginning of the process of writing it.

Praise for previous works by Jonathan Rutherford

I am No Longer Myself Without You: An Anatomy of Love (Flamingo 2000)
'A neatly perceptive, likeable, highly salutary meditation on the nature of male love'
Felix Benjamin, *Mail on Sunday*

'Intriguing... Rutherford is master of his chosen subject, masculinity',
Paul Johnson, *Sunday Telegraph*

'A superior, cogent, fascinating study, argued convincingly',
Tim Teeman, *New Statesman*

Male Order (Lawrence & Wishart 1988)
'a stylish and perceptive exploration of the territories of contemporary masculinity and its many disavowals'
Stuart Hall

Forever England (Lawrence & Wishart 1997)
'a courageous step towards the understanding and affirmation of a new English identity ... radical, readable and important'
Mike Phillips

Identity: Community, Culture, Difference (Lawrence & Wishart 1990)
'brings clarity of thought to a situation which I don't think I am alone in finding confusing'
Roger Baker, *Gay Times*

Soundings

'Soundings helps to keep my faith in an intellectual left alive. In a world of shrinking media outlets for serious reflection about what's going on and what can be done about it, Soundings consistently challenges my assumptions and opens my mind to new questions, ideas and possibilities.'

Lawrence Grossberg,
Professor of Communication
Studies and Cultural Studies,
University of North Carolina
at Chapel Hill

Editor: Jonathan Rutherford
Founding editors: Stuart Hall, Doreen Massey, Michael Rustin

For more information about Soundings
write to **Soundings, Freepost, Lon 15823, London E9 5BR**
(no stamp needed)
email sally@lwbooks.co.uk
visit the Soundings website www.soundings.org.uk